DAYBREAK

"Unforgettable overtones of a truly sensitive artist linger on long after the last page. Perhaps this is because the author sensed that for all the autobiographical passages — about her Mexican intellectual father and her strange but beautiful mother, her family's constant uprooting from town to town—she was not so much writing her own story as orchestrating her experience with youth, with the so-called generation gap, and with the nonviolent protest movement ... DAYBREAK is a kind of tender hymn to this generation's sound of silence."

Newsweek

DAYBREAK

"In poetic prose, Joan Baez talks about the people, experiences, ideas and ideals that have shaped her life. She includes a good look at herself as a young girl growing up with her fears; a glowing tribute to her mother; an analysis of her father and of her relationship with him; and brief glimpses of Ira, her spiritual mentor, of Richard Farina ... and of David, her husband, who faces a jail term for refusing military service. Her compassion, honesty, and sincerity come through here loud and clear."

Library Journal

DAYBREAK

"Her sketches of her family, friends, and a lover are precise, often witty and without a tinge of pretentiousness. . . . Pulsing hard through it all is the beat of life —the strong vibrato that characterizes Joan Baez's singing. The book is uncategorizable, as is Joan herself; and they are both celebrations of life."

Playboy

"A beautifully written, insightful book that should warm even the stoniest heart."

Book-of-the-Month Club News

DAYBREAK

JOAN BAEZ

AVON
PUBLISHERS OF
DISCUS · CAMELOT · BARD

"Child of Darkness" first published in *Esquire*, September 1966 under the title "Introduction to (and Conclusion of) a Future Hero."

AVON BOOKS
A division of
The Hearst Corporation
959 Eighth Avenue
New York, New York 10019

First Printing, June, 1969
Sixth Printing, October, 1970

AVON TRADEMARK REG. U.S. PAT. OFF. AND FOREIGN COUNTRIES, REGISTERED TRADEMARK— MARCA REGISTRADA, HECHO EN CHICAGO, U.S.A.

Printed in the U.S.A.

This book is dedicated with love, admiration, and gratefulness to the men who find themselves facing imprisonment for resisting the draft.

Contents

DAYBREAK

DREAM

I was watching a carnival from a distance, watching thousands of colored balloons, little ones crammed into huge ones, every color, all filled with helium, when suddenly the balloons broke loose and began floating upwards. There was a child hanging from each big balloon, about three children in all, and everyone screamed, "Hang on," and I wondered how in hell they would get those children down. They floated over the land towards the sea, and the balloons began popping. A huge carnival ride was pushed out into the sea, and jets came over and police cars were ready in the water and children were tearing about planning to catch the floaters when they hit the water. I remember wondering if they wouldn't get smothered under popped balloons before anyone could get to them. I think they made it OK into a police car, down a ramp of the carnival ride, into the ocean and were towed through the water to safety.

SCHOOL

Mother tells me that I came back from the first day of kindergarten and told her I was in love. I remember a Japanese boy who looked after me and wouldn't let anybody knock me around. When they gave us beans to eat in the morning I told him they'd make me sick, and he buried them under the table for me.

A Saint Bernard tried to play with me one afternoon and he rolled me down the hill. I was so terrified that I wet my pants.

There was a boy who drank milk with me. He picked flowers a lot, and I always wanted to pat his head. The kids called him a she-she boy.

I usually ran home in the morning with a stomach ache and got in bed and listened to Babar or Uncle Don's Nursery Rhymes. Once when I was sick Arthur Foster Bevelockway fell off the banister and knocked his front teeth out. I fell in love with him.

We moved.

I hated first grade. I hated "Red Rover, Red Rover, Let Joanie Come Over," because it was easy to get hurt, and because I hated to be on a losing side, so I'd do anything, even cheat, to win.

One morning in second grade I ran to the girls' room and hung my head over the toilet to be sick; the teacher held my head but nothing happened. I think that was during arithmetic. The next time it happened I know it was during arithmetic. Pretty soon it was worked out that I could go to the teacher's room whenever I felt sick. I loved that. I could fall asleep. It was next best to being home.

One day I found a treasure. It was a silver keychain, about one foot long. The kind you close by pushing the last little ball at each end into a silver latch. I stayed after school by myself and threw the chain up in the air over and over, watching it flash and glisten in the sun. I lay down in the deserted schoolyard and dropped the chain into my mouth and pulled it out all wet, whirling it around over my head until it was freezing cold and then lowering it onto my forehead in loop designs . . . Ecstasy. The afternoon ended in tragedy when I threw the chain in the air and it landed on the school roof. I was too stunned even to cry. And when I went to get my sweater there was a bumblebee on it and I was afraid to pick it up. I tried to reason with the bee, and then tried to shoo it away from a safe distance of three feet and finally, in a state of perfect terror and guilt, I stepped on it and ground my foot into the sweater to be sure the bee was dead.

About that time my career with men began to get really active. I remember chasing a Japanese boy around the entire schoolyard—under jungle-gyms and around swings. When I finally caught up to him he had stopped running and seemed to be staggering in slow motion. He was holding the top of his head and blood was mixed with the dust on his hands. He had cracked his head open on the metal merry-go-round. He was absent for a few days, and came back to school with a round spot shaved in the middle of his thick black hair and some dark stitches showing on a very white scalp. I felt guilty about him.

I found a snake one day and decided to stuff it the way they do in museums, so I got all the proper equipment: scissors, a bucket of water to keep things clean, some cotton for the stuffing and a needle and thread to sew it up. I became discouraged after his innards were all floating around in the bucket, and I figured he'd never look too good anyway, since his head had been run over to begin with, so I gave up and ripped a dead gopher apart with the neighbor boy. He took the head and I took the tail and we pulled. I did it to show how tough I could be, and to make my sister sick. She got sick and we put the gopher remains in a paper bag and left it behind the house.

I was the fastest runner in second grade. I knew how to draw a cow with huge udders and a tepee and a rooster standing on the right-

16

hand side of the page with "Cock-a-doodle-doo" coming out of his beak from right to left in mirror writing. I envied everything about my older sister, Pauline, including the patch she had to wear over one eye, and I didn't care if my little sister, Mimi, lived or died. I had a beautiful dress that was red velvet on top and plaid satin on the bottom, which Mother finally let me wear to school, and I was the first person in the whole school to come down with pink eye. I loved the Sons of the Pioneers and Tex Ritter and "Last night I heard the wild goose cry" by Frankie Laine. I was crazy for fast vibratos. My mother passed by me in the kitchen one time and smoothed my forehead and said, "You look as if you were carrying the whole world on your shoulders." Once in the middle of the night I heard "The Star-Spangled Banner," and I stood up in bed in my nightie and saluted until it was finished because I thought that's what you were supposed to do.

We moved.

Third grade was in the East. I got straight A's. A boy named Michael and I were the smartest ones in our class, and the time I got straight A's he got one A minus. He took it hard. Winter was a big thing for us kids. It snowed on Christmas Eve. We hung onto car bumpers after dinner when it was dark and slid on the ice for blocks. We used to sneak across the street and watch television through the neighbor's window—Kooklafrananolly. It was a small-minded little town, and one night the neighbors ran a wire from tree to tree around

17

the entire house. As we were running across the yard to the bushes, I got it in the neck. The wire knocked me down and I lost my wind and hurt my head.

Another neighbor didn't like niggers or Mexicans or professors or kids, and I wasn't allowed on his lawn. Pauline was, because she was light.

The old lady next door lived with an old man who wasn't her husband and who didn't ever wear his teeth. The old lady's son was a criminal, and she kept his daughter. One night he came to town to claim his little girl. He was drunk and he had a knife and he backed the old lady, his mother, against the kitchen wall and said he was going to slit her open from here to here. She got out of it by telling him she had to go to the bathroom. One night Pauline and Mimi and the old lady's granddaughter and I were out in the old man's pigpen dumping things on the pig's head and getting nervous that we'd be caught, and in the middle of our whispering and hysterical giggles came a blinding flash of lightning followed almost immediately by a crack of thunder, which sounded as if it had come right from the pigpen. We didn't stop to look at each other. Home had never been so many paces away.

An evangelist came to town one spring. Mother took us kids to see him. He sang:

> Get the new look from the old book,
> Get the new look from the Bible.

All the women in town went to his meetings. I liked him—until he pointed at me and told me to pray out loud. I couldn't do it.

I was the school veterinarian, and the kids brought me all their animals when they were sick or even dead. I would draw pictures of the dead ones first and then bury them. One Friday I left a Baltimore oriole in my school desk, and on Monday the teacher walked into class and nearly fainted from the smell. I didn't know what the smell was until I opened my desk. It was pretty terrible. I'd never seen maggots before and I felt bad about the bird. I drew pictures of all of Disney's characters and sold them to the kids for two cents apiece. I lined the pennies up in the groove which was cut out for pencils.

I had a great friend named Lily. She was some weird religion, and her parents wouldn't let her cut her hair. She lived on a farm across from a pea cannery, and Lily and I slept up in her hayloft. She could yodel and she said her S's so clearly that they almost whistled, and her chin moved in a way that I could watch for hours. At the end of fourth grade she gave me a going-away present. It was a chopped-off chicken leg with the tendons all sticking out so that you could pull them and make the claws move separately. I kept it until it rotted.

There was a very poor and raggedy girl who lived just out of town, almost on top of the railroad tracks. She was thin and shy and unhealthy-looking and wore all hand-me-downs. She had no friends at all, and I used to go and

19

play with her baby pigs. At the end of the year I went around to all the kids and their parents to collect money. I got thirteen dollars and Mother helped me get her a dress and some shoes and socks and a hair ribbon. She didn't know what was happening when the class presented her with the presents. I think she cried.

We moved.

In fifth grade we were in Southern California. There was a big black boy who looked after me. He was the first person to come up and say hello on the playground. He told me if there was anything I needed just to let him know. A bunch of Mexican girls said they were going to beat me up on the way home from school, so I told David, and he walked me home every day until it was safe. There were three Nancys and two Carols in my class. I wasn't very popular because I was a new kid again and because I was a Mexican. I was skinny and very brown. I had a crush on Andy Crane, but he had a crush on my best friend, Sharon, and they used to kiss in the coat room after school and I would stand there and count for them. Count how long the kiss was.

I loved my teacher. He was the best elementary-school teacher I ever had. His name was MacIntosh and we called him Mr. Mac. I think he liked me. One day in the schoolyard I called someone a son of a bitch at the top of my lungs and Mr. Mac called me in. He said, "I suppose you know what I have to talk to you about?" and I said, "If it's about what I said at recess, we both know that a bitch is a she-dog and there's nothing wrong with saying it," and he smiled. He made me feel as though we could understand, but the other kids couldn't, so I never said it again. He had a smooth forehead and pretty eyes.

I was still a fast runner, and when we had the big inter-school track meet, I would have won the footrace but this tall skinny super-athlete girl from another school entered at the last minute. Her teachers pushed her into the starting line at my place, which had little starting foot-blocks, and I had to take another place with no foot-blocks. I ran like the wind but could only come in second. She did the same thing at standing broad jump, and I got another red ribbon. She was a sixth-grader and not supposed to compete in our class. I could have killed her.

I thought I was kind of funny looking, but my mother and father said I had a million-dollar smile. For my tenth birthday they gave me a collie. It was too good to believe. He was just a puppy and we called him Professor Wooley. He had an especially long nose when he grew up, and a way of talking to me from his throat. I don't think he was very smart, but it was like a wonderful movie having my own dog. And it ended the way all of those movies end. Goodbye, Professor Wooley . . .

We moved.

This time we were going to Baghdad, Iraq. We stopped overnight in a hotel in Lebanon and the shower and sink and wall toilet were all in one closet. You could go to the bathroom and take a shower at the same time. We didn't sleep much because it was hot and the sounds were so foreign. My father and his flock had never smelled anything like those smells. The next day, on the way to the airport bus, I was running my hand along a park fence and all of a sudden there was bare flesh under my hand. It was the swollen tummy of a half-naked beggar boy. The airplane from Lebanon to Baghdad was flown by Middle Eastern Airways and it was hot in the front and freezing in the back, and filled with flies. The first thing we saw when we landed in Baghdad was an old beggar being beaten and poked at by the police. It put my soul in anguish. We stayed at the Semiramis Hotel and all got diarrhea. I watched Arab men in their pretty robes eat rice and lamb with their hands. They were very graceful with their hands, but their faces were coarse and ugly. We saw round boats floating down the Tigris. One time we saw a dead horse doing the same thing. He looked like a balloon made of hide. We stayed at the YMCA for a while and I ate rice cakes and dates and threw up. We were all pretty sick. Pauline lived in the bathroom for about three days and we finally had to call a doctor. The doctor was a big mannish woman who said we must eat lebon, which was yogurt, but I wouldn't touch it and I think we eventually stayed alive on the mashed bananas. I had jaundice too. They took me to the hospital three times and I finally showed the doctor my palms and the soles of my feet and explained that the reason they were yellow was because I had jaundice and he said, "Oh, you think so?" I was getting sicker and sicker and the last time we went they took blood from my arm and when I tried to get up and walk I fainted in a chair. They said, "Bring her back tomorrow and we'll see what the tests tell us." My mother said, "No. You get her a bed here. Now." They got me one. "Second floor, madam," said the doctor. "You carry her. She's not taking another step." Someone carried me and put me in a bed. Later that day I asked to be moved to the bed near the window and they moved me and made up the old bed without changing the sheets. I now looked out over the main street in town. Al Rashid Street. I could look down and see red double-decker English buses and skinny horses, and camels; there was an overwhelming smell of exhaust. Once I saw a man carrying a piano on his back. After two days in the hospital I asked them if they could give me a bath and two giggling Arab nurses came in and washed me, all but my private parts, which they kept covered with a towel. I got so angry I sent them out of the room and washed myself. Mother brought me home. I was very sick for a long time. When I was on my feet again I saw some amazing things. Women came to eat out of our garbage can. I wrapped up some cake once and put it in the garbage. I watched a woman open the package and frown. She didn't know what it was. I tried to motion to her to eat it, but she wouldn't. I guess she just didn't trust me.

Once I gave a crazy old beggar lady some

coins. She put them in her mouth. I had no food on me so I gave her my Chiclets. She took them out of the box and put the box in her mouth.

There was a big wall around our house. In the next yard a family lived in a mud hut. The children had one robe apiece for clothing, and when one washed his robe, he went naked until it was dry.

My father was having a Quaker meeting in the house one day and I didn't want to interrupt it, but the neighbors on the left side of our house were beating a puppy to death in an upstairs window. They had him cornered in the screen, which was caving out, and they were stoning him. I screamed at them in Arabic to give me the dog and they thought that was a real joke. He died, probably of fright. I've seldom known such anguish. I looked after all the dogs in the neighborhood. The dog across the street was named Tarzan. He belonged to the servant girl. When she'd call him he'd run up, wagging his tail, then crouch to the ground and cower. She'd kick him in the head. I think he loved her anyway. It was all they knew. One day the master of the house called Tarzan over and when the dog crouched in front of him, the man shot him in the head and killed him. I was happy.

That same awful man brought us some pigeons for a gift. He said they'd make good pets, only you had to cut their wings. We said, oh no, we liked them better with their wings on, but he was suspicious, and he sat right there, talking and clipping their wings in front of us. Pauline and Mimi and I looked at each other in sorrow and exasperation. We put the birds on the roof, where we planned to keep them until their wings grew back, and then let them go. But the big terrible Bull-bull birds attacked and killed one of the pigeons and pecked the other's eyes out. I saw it first and was almost hysterical with hate for the Bull-bulls and agony for the pigeons. We built a little house for the bird that was left, but in his blindness he wandered out into the sun and was also killed. Now I think that a child might be reading this and I won't tell any more painful things. Just that the dog I loved best, named Findick, knew that we were leaving Baghdad, and while Pauline packed all the trunks, because Mother was sick, Findick sat and watched us and quit wagging his tail. Every night as I was going to sleep on the flat roof of our house, I would pray to the Big Dipper that Findick would die so he couldn't suffer when we'd gone . . . And now I know that he must be dead, because all of that happened seventeen years ago, and dogs over there have short lives, to say nothing of the people.

We left Baghdad.

We went to Switzerland for a month, where I drank too much milk because we hadn't had real milk in eight months. Wild strawberries grew around the chalet where we lived. We stayed for a while in a place where they didn't allow liquor. One day Pauline and Mimi and some friends we'd met and I ran off to play in

25

the woods. We were playing Follow the Leader, and Pauline noticed a man watching us from behind a tree . . . Every time we looked back at him he had moved a little closer, and it was getting very spooky. We were about to take off for home when I thought of a plan. We ran up to him and danced around him like Indians and then stopped and puffed on a big stick and handed it to him saying, "Smokum peace pipe." He went away.

We visited Rome for two days and went on a bus tour to the Vatican and some museums. I was so tired that I held Mother's hand and walked along with my eyes closed and asked her to tell me if there was anything especially pretty and I would look. I woke up for the Sistine Chapel.

We moved back to Southern California. The big black boy was still there to look after me. And the problem with the Mexicans was still there. I became best friends with a girl who was Mexican but refused to speak Spanish. She did everything that she could to be like the popular kids. I was jealous of her because she had fifteen stick-out slips, and I had three, which I wore every day and ironed with wax paper at night to make them stiff again.

I wore undershirts until the girls, trying to be nice, asked me when I would start wearing a bra. I was completely flat-chested but bought the tiniest bra made and stuffed it with all sorts of things to pad it up . . . Kleenex and bits of material. I worried constantly about the rings under my eyes, and some days I wouldn't go to school because I thought I looked so awful. My socks belled at the top and I had a forehead full of pimples. My parents went on saying that I had a million-dollar smile. I thought that it was all I had. Mother always told me I was much better than pretty but my father didn't understand that I needed to hear something aside from the fact that I had a million-dollar smile.

Eighth grade was the same as seventh. We had a nice girls' principal. She was fat and kind and let me go home when I was too down to stand it. Some of the popular kids were kind to me. They all *liked* me, but it was a risk for them to treat me as anything aside from sort of a witty court jester when we were in public.

I was the best artist in school and when school elections came around I made posters for everyone I knew. I even made them for both the guys who were running for president. That's how badly I wanted to have friends, and that's how much I cared about class officers.

In the middle of all that hell there was a man who threw me a lifeline. He was our family doctor. He told me I could come to his office whenever I wanted. Just walk in. One time I left class and walked to his office. I hadn't eaten anything solid for about three days. I was living on a sick, hot and cold energy. He told me I was not ill, and he gave me a pill which he said would help me relax. He said just to rest there as long as I wanted and if I needed him, to call. Then he went off to see his other patients.

Half an hour later I was starving hungry, and about that time he walked in with a milk-shake and a hamburger and took time to talk to me. He told me that I was not ordinary pretty, but beautiful. He said that the girls at school whom I envied so much were burning them-selves out. Just when they had burned them-selves completely out, I would be starting to show that I was something special. I said yeah, but what about the rings under my eyes, and he said they were very fashionable, that women paid money to make their eyes dark like that. He said I was beautiful. And that was the be-ginning of the end of my childhood and the be-ginning of the end of the sorrow that came with seeing myself as a skinny brown friendly knock-kneed flat-chested artistic bold black-haired outcast with a million-dollar smile.

MARISA

How can I describe to you the way Marisa picked wildflowers in the valley? Her sweater was as pink as the sunset, and her little red shoes of patent leather slipped on the grassy hill.

MY MOTHER

She can't stand anything phony. She refuses to go to teas, prefers young people to older. She works in the garden, making flowers come up out of the dirt. She wears her hair long, down her back when she's at home, and up in a braided roll when she goes out. Her back is strong and her hands are gnarly and full of veins. I think she must have worked very hard when she was little to have such hands. Her eyes are huge, frightened, deep, and magnificent; her forehead almost always in a worry design; her mouth too tight and her chin tense. Yet there is an overwhelming strength in her face, and she is one of about five women I can think of who are in her category of beauty. Her figure is excellent. When she runs, on the beach, dressed in blue jeans and a T-shirt, with her hair all down, she looks nineteen. She is fifty-four.

Mother was born in Scotland, and brought to America when she was two. Her mother died when she was three. Her father was a very far-out Episcopalian minister who loved the theater, sang off-key from the pulpit, dressed his children out of the missionary barrel, fought a fiery public battle with the DAR, and had a weakness for marrying domineering women. Mother says I would have loved him. I can think of only one picture of him, a portrait showing a weak, thin-nosed, rather nice-looking sad man. There comes to mind now a picture of Mother's mother, carrying Mother's sister on her back: She is very pretty, also sad, tilting her head back as though to bump it in a nice way against the baby's head. Now I think of the picture of Mother which I have hanging in my house. It was taken when she was ten. She is standing on a beach in the wind with the ocean in back of her, her arms outstretched in youthful grace, her dark legs poking out of an oversized black bathing costume, coming a bit together at the knees, the wind blowing her hair across her face, across an exquisite smile. Her head is tilted back, as though butting the wind. She is like a lovely bit of dark heather. She has kept the grace and beauty through unbelievable odds. Odds which have given her a power and wisdom which she tries very hard not to acknowledge.

Her first stepmother was classically frigid, and appears dressed in white, smiling very sweetly, in all the old albums. She's the one who would hand Mother and her sister fifteen cents and say, "Here's your allowance for this week," and before they could close their fingers over the coins, she'd say, "and now, because you've spilled the ink in the study and made a mess in the john and stolen peanut butter from the big jar, I am taking it away. Maybe you can learn to be good children, and then you will get your allowance." Money was dirty to touch, Jews were dirty to live near, sex was dirty to think about or have; children were taught by punishment; and in the meantime dressing everyone in white frocks would tide things over. Long before I learned these things, she was a favorite "auntie" of my childhood. She let go her grip long enough to produce a son, a half-brother for Mother and her sister to look after. He grew up to be a Right-wing fanatic, made it through medical school to become a urologist on sheer strength of will because his mother told him he was too stupid to pass the exams. I hear he's a good doctor.

The next stepmother was a six-foot-tall redhead schizophrenic who made puppets and dressed in purple and orange and was prone to chasing Mother's father around the house waving a butcher knife and screaming. Mother once ran to her father's church, entered in the middle of the Sunday sermon. She reached the pulpit and stood there anxiously in her funny missionary clothing, waiting for her kindly but oblivious father to stop his ranting long enough to notice her. When he didn't, she leaned forward and caught his eye and said, "Daddy, please, you must come. Meg's beating up Pauline." "Heavens!" he said, sweeping down from the pulpit, and rushing out of the church. He arrived home too late, as Meg had dragged Mother's older sister around by the hair, beaten and kicked her until she was unrecognizable and locked her in her room.

Meg's sadistic energies were centered on the older sister, because of her closeness to her father, and Mother was more often than not just ignored.

She declared her independence when she was thirteen. Meg threw a pot of steaming boiled potatoes at her from across the room. Mother ducked the potatoes and went about washing the dishes. Meg came up behind her and slapped her full strength on the side of the face. Mother whirled around and said, "Damn you!" and Meg froze in shock. When she regained her fury she raised her arms to beat Mother, but Mother caught her arms mid-flight with her own slippery hands, and lowered them to her sides, saying, "Don't you ever do that again." Meg fumbled in her defeat, and finally said, "Go outside and fill this up with berries," handing Mother a pot, and Mother said, "If you want berries, pick them yourself." From then on Mother kept her coat hanging near the front door, with two nickels in the pocket, one for bus fare, and the other to call a friend.

At some point in her childhood she lived in a sort of gypsy camp for a while, eating potato crusts charcoaled in the fire on sticks. She and her little friends ate them because there wasn't much food around and no one bothered to feed

33

the children. She found communion wafers delightful, but not very filling. And she *was* guilty of stealing peanut butter—she would steal it in great globs, knowing that she would eventually be caught and punished. She's not hungry like that any more, but she still has a craving for peanut butter.

There was one school she was sent to which she loved. They left her alone there, and she could sit by a brook and not go to class. She was good in drama and wanted to act, but the ghosts of stepmothers, sweetly and regretfully explaining to her that she was inadequate in every way and not very bright, kept her from pursuing anything beyond the first few steps. It was the same with nursing. She loves it, and is brilliant with sick people, but she never got beyond being a nurse's aide.

She has told me of when she was left in charge of a dying girl. The child had been in an accident, and was fatally hurt, and Mother was supposed to mark down the exact time of her death. She watched the little girl struggle, and give, and struggle again, always fading, and always in pain. When her small muscles sank into the hospital bed for the last time, Mother felt very deeply the blessing of that final defeat.

Her father by blindness to his children, and the stepmothers out of jealousy and the etiquette of the times, convinced Mother that she was not pretty. When she and her sister were little their hair was pulled tightly back and braided, lest anyone should notice that Pauline had soft yellow curls, and Mother had shiny handsome brown hair. Still, in every picture I've seen of her when she was young, she is nothing less than strikingly beautiful.

In a snapshot taken of her when she was about eighteen she stands sideways to the camera, dressed in satin, with some feathery shawl around her shoulders, her eyes looking into the lens. She is a vamp, a gypsy queen, a mystic, a blueblood. She is all of those things still, and the battle rages inside and outside Mother as to whether she will ever admit to the fact that she is glorious.

I have said little specifically about Mother's mind. There is little to say, as she refused to acknowledge its existence, let alone its depth and brilliance. My guess is that it will continue to remain an almost totally untapped uranium deposit.

Mother knows nothing of the theories of mysticism, but it seems as if God moves about her more freely than He does most people, and that the soul of Mother is in some way so familiar with His presence that she doesn't think to title their relationship. There is a spookiness which comes with that side of Mother—the kind of spookiness which provides demons for her dreams, and sometimes accompanies them to her bedroom window. "Oh I remember! It wasn't a dream. It was Kit. She came to the window in the form of a ghastly angel, and leaned in over the bed and flapped her wings. I couldn't speak to ask her what she wanted, and

35

I wished she would leave, because she was horrible, and I was scared to death."

I think now of the stories Mother has told me of Meg setting an extra place at the table for a deceased member of the family. Namely, Mother's real mother. Meg would give her a plate of food, and say to the children, "Shhhh. Elizabeth has something to say." And they would stare at the empty chair while Meg nodded and spoke, sympathetically pausing to listen and respond. The ghost never ate her dinner.

The family lived for a while in a big house in the woods a few miles from a men's prison. Escapees came often to the house looking for food, and Mother and her sister were often alone and frightened. At night they fought because there was a candle to light the room, and Mother couldn't go to sleep if it was lit because she was afraid of fire, and Pauline wouldn't blow it out because she was afraid of the dark.

Mother and me. Tea and Vivaldi and Mozart and Jussi Bjoerling singing Puccini . . . comfort at home from the misery at school. "Is there anything important you should be doing at school?" "No," I would say, and the nice thing was that both Mother and I knew that nothing very important was ever going to happen at school. The habit of running home in the morning began when I was in first grade. Mother delivered me to a new school, and left me in line with thirty other kids, waiting for the bell. I didn't know if I was in the right line, and a huge empty feeling was growing in my stomach, and my chest was beginning to tighten, and instead of asking someone which line was for first-graders, I tied my sweater sleeves in a knot around my waist and ran home. It was easy enough to find my house, because it was the only place in the world I wanted to be. I don't remember if Mother made me go back that time. Probably not.

In 1951, the year we spent in Baghdad, Iraq, after an explosive two weeks of trying to adjust to a French-English Catholic school, during which time the three disruptive Baez girls broke every rule that had ever been written for that school, and I had presented a case for some new rules to be written, Mother said, "Oh for heaven's sake," and took me out of school for the rest of that year. I stayed home and did things. I made cakes—real ones, not out of a box. I learned about ants by carefully digging into their hills and finding the nursery and transplanting bunches of unborn babies and nurses and workers into a huge treacle bottle filled with dirt. The trick was to try and find a queen, and then watch them establish a new colony. I sprayed scorpions with DDT until they were groggy, and picked them up and put them in matchboxes to get a closer look at them, with their scary spiked tails, and to draw pictures of them. I didn't know they were poisonous. I was commissioned by my father to make large ink drawings of some pictures of cells and hair follicles and epidermal tissue as seen through a microscope, for a biology professor at the University of Baghdad. I studied flies under my father's microscope, and drew pictures in colored pencil of their wings and legs and eyes. I made miniature houses out of mud and twigs, two and three stories high. And every morning, around ten, Mother and I would sit in the back yard, in the sun, and eat oranges and have some tea, and maybe some of the cake I had made, and I'd show her my projects. She always appreciated everything. I didn't realize until now the creativity that was let out of chains when Mother gave me that year of freedom.

It is worth mentioning the three months I was sick that same year. There were times when I felt that if I wasn't in Mother's hands, I would float off toward the vicinity of death.

Mother was never out of earshot when things were at the worst. Once I was in such a high fever, and so weak, that I thought I would simply die of heat. I wanted a sip of lemonade which was in a glass by my bed. I had the choice of reaching down for it, which seemed impossibly difficult to do, or calling for Mother, who sat reading twenty feet away. I took a deep breath and let it make a noise on the way out. Mother was by the bed by the time I'd breathed all the way out, saying, "You want some lemonade, honey?" She sat through days of my fits of diarrhea, holding my head and rubbing my back as I sweated and cried and shook on the cold little potty, which she then had to empty downstairs. I remember apologizing to her about the smell, telling her she didn't

have to stay, but praying she wouldn't leave
. . . She never left.

Once in that time I had a dream which was
so vivid that I called Mother in to tell her. I
dreamed I was riding a bicycle across an empty
plain, on a road which began to get smaller and
smaller and full of potholes, until eventually I
couldn't even ride, but had to guide the bike
with my feet and coast. I came to the edge of
the plain, and there was a drop-off into a great
canyon, and on the other side of the canyon
was a beautiful field of green grass. I didn't
stop to deliberate, but gave the bicycle a good
push with my foot, and sailed over the cliff toward the lovely field. I woke up as I was floating through the air. Mother listened to the
dream and nodded, and years later told me she
thought I had meant to die then. It was during
those months that I had a split of about a quarter of an inch in my life-line, and the only way
I could make the line come together was by
stretching the skin over the split until there was
a faint red line showing. I was too embarrassed
and frightened to tell even Mother that I
thought it meant I would die soon. The line has
grown back so completely that it is impossible
to tell where the split once was.

Though Mother and I admit that she must
have been, in part, responsible for helping
build my house of fears, she was one of the few
people who had the key to get me out. Does
that mean she must have put me in? Perhaps.
But she and her sister Pauline, and my sister
Mimi, were the only ones who knew how to

push the terror aside when it was enveloping me. I can see that pushing it aside cures nothing, but by age five the fears were so solid that I had already become a genius at running from them, and running like that is a hard habit to break. Mother nursed me through terror from that early age until I moved out of the house at age nineteen. Perhaps the blows of adolescence made junior high and early high school the roughest time.

"It will pass. It always passes. Take a deep breath. Another one. That's right. There, can you feel that breeze?" I would grip her hand with all my strength, and imagine that her blood was flowing into my veins and giving me energy. I shut my eyes and saw a chart with a graph on it, and while I was at the worst part I could see the line dip below the bottom of the page, and then I knew it would start up again. I breathed deeply, through my nose, the way anyone does when he's trying to keep from throwing up, and then, eventually, as Mother said, it would begin to go away. "You're getting better now," she'd say. "I can feel it in your hands." I would always come out joking. When the line on the graph was up to safety level, my first impulse was to ridicule the whole thing, and then Mother would go off to put on the tea kettle, and sometimes I would be asleep before she got back. Each bout like that used up all my strength, and left me dazed and exhausted, and sometimes, after the really big ones, in a queer melancholy sort of state. And each time when it was over I'd put it aside in my mind and forget, or not care that there would be another. But now I think how Mother must have suffered through all that, wondering what had brought it about and why her little girl should have to carry such a strange load . . . and, no doubt, how she must be to blame.

My mother's been to jail with me twice now. We did civil disobedience together at the Oakland induction center. She told me she didn't know if it would do any good, but that it might give other mothers some courage to do the same, or something just as radical. It did. Our second trip to Santa Rita Prison there were at least three women in with us who said that Mother had given them the strength to act out their convictions.

Mother really hated it in jail, because it was so easy for her, and so unfair to the regular inmates. The black dope addicts and prostitutes and boosters and pushers called her "Mama." Whenever they swore in front of her they said, " 'Scuse me, Mama." On Christmas Day, one of the three toughest girls in the women's side of the prison came to Mother's bed and said, "Ooooo, Mama. Ah'm down. They doin' it to me. Ah'm *way* down. I wanna see mah kids. An I don't *never* cry. But I b'lieve I'm gone have to today!" and she folded up in Mother's arms and shook her head and cried. Mother patted her black angora hairdo and kissed her on the forehead and said softly but angrily "Yeah. It's all pretty rotten, isn't it. Just plain stinking."

We were sprung from jail two weeks early.

The jailers were afraid of the uproar which might ensue when we were to say good-bye to our friends, so they didn't tell us we were going home until a half hour before we left. We sat in the Lieutenant's office, and talked to her. Mother had never spent any time with this woman. She asked if she could go back to the building where she had been working and say good-bye to her friends.

"No," said the Lieutenant.

"But I have to say good-bye to Gladys," said Mother.

"I'm sorry, but I'm afraid you can't."

"You're not sorry," I said, "and you know we can. If you'll let us."

"Are you asking for special privileges, Joan?"

"Sure, if that's a special privilege. I didn't notice that it was. Everyone around here gets to say good-bye . . ."

"I won't leave until I've said good-bye to Gladys and Jean," said Mother. The Lieutenant changed the subject.

"You know, I've never had the time to really speak with you, Mrs. Baez. It's a pity, because you look like an interesting person."

"Well," said Mother. "I'm glad I came here. I think I've learned a lot. In fact I know I have. Stuff I could never have learned anywhere else."

The Lieutenant brightened. "Really?" she said. "What have you learned?"

"Oh," said Mother, looking at the Lieutenant from under her contraband eye makeup, "I know how to steal now. I think I could steal about anything, if it was necessary. I can smuggle. I can get all sorts of stuff into the cells."

The Lieutenant looked jarred and suspicious. Mother went on. "I never thought I would be able to lie. In fact I've never been able to lie, all my life. But now I find that I can look someone right in the eye and tell a bold-faced lie. It's not so hard if it's for someone who's locked up and not being treated well . . ."

"Are you serious?" said the Lieutenant.

"Oh yes," said Mother. "It's marvelous . . ."

I butted in. "So you're letting us out of here on good behavior, is that it?"

"To be truthful with you, Joan, it was not my idea to let you go. I would not have recommended you for good time." She turned to Mother. "You know, Mrs. Baez, I don't think jail is a good place for your daughter. She has a tendency to, well, kind of fit in awfully fast . . . I could see her easily beginning to fall into some of the patterns that the regular inmates have formed, and you know, whether we like it or not, we are dealing with two very different classes here. . ."

"What are you trying to say?" I asked her.

"Well it just doesn't seem like a good atmosphere for you, some of the habits that—"

"She's afraid I'm going to turn queer," I said to Mother with a smile.

"Oh heavens," Mother laughed. "My daughter's been queer for years. Don't let that bother you. She got it from me."

We ended our chat right about then, and all the deputies and sergeants began hustling us to

43

get processed and out before the prison grapevine had spread the news that Mama and Joan Junior were being sprung. They kept rushing us, and I kept telling Mother to take her time, that they had no right to rush us. So we ironed our crumpled streetclothes, and distributed all our candy and skin lotion and stamps, and the grapevine began to hum, and within fifteen minutes our most beloved and devoted friends made it through two locked doors and past the Lieutenant's office to the ironing room to embrace us and kiss us good-bye, and then to vanish down the starched but internally crumbling hallways of Santa Rita. And Mother hit the damp chilly morning on the outside with a labeled Santa Rita kitchen apron stuffed under her pea jacket, and fourteen letters tucked into her long winter underwear.

I went by my parents' house at seven o'clock this morning on the way home from the airport. The sky was gray, and the ground wet. There are some iron cowbells hanging at the second gate, and inside the gate, in the yard, Mother was digging up some ground around a big tree stump. She always looks surprised when I walk up, and she said, "Oh, how nice," and put down her shovel. She had made some applesauce, soup, and banana bread for me to take home, since I don't cook anymore. I went down to my father's study to say hello, and we began a long chat about a ship—an idea for an international university ship, with international students, to travel all over the world. There were pictures

44

of Mother all over the room. We got around to talking about her, as we usually do, my father and I, and he showed me a picture I hadn't seen for a long time. "It's not very good, technically," he was saying, "but it's kind of a sweet expression, don't you think?" At the edge of his desk apart from the piles of papers and science pamphlets and correspondence was a copy of the complicity statement which, once signed, puts the signer in the position of having aided and abetted draft resisters. He knows that Mother has been considering signing it, and that it could mean she would go to jail for some time. "That's the nice thing about Mum's position you know, she is really free to pick up and leave if she feels it's necessary," he said, and cleared his throat.

DREAM

Walking up my hill and a tiny foreign car came roaring and sliding up in the dust with two middle-aged lesbians in it. I pushed it from behind because it was skidding around in a rut, and we got it up the hill. The road was different and so was my house, with the usual array of dream people making themselves at home all over the front yard. The arches were about three feet high, and people were sitting on them. I caught up with the two women, the car having gained speed on the flat area of the hill, and was going to ask them what they wanted, when the driver stormed out of the car and towards the front door with her friend, not quite so abruptly, following. "Hey," I said, "you want something?" But they kept charging forward, and went in the house (it was a different house completely by then—more like the one here in Hawaii). I got sort of angry and

46

shouted, "Where the hell do you think you're going?" and ran after them.

By the time I caught up, the aggressive one was opening all the kitchen closets and drawers, searching frantically for something. "What does she *want?*" I asked the quiet one. "She's looking for a bag of tonsils she left here," she replied. I said I didn't think there was a bag of tonsils anywhere in the house, but I'd call and check with Susie.

MY FATHER

My father is short, honest, dark, and very handsome. He's good, he's a good man. He was born in Mexico, and brought up in Brooklyn. His father was a Mexican who left the Catholic church to become a Methodist minister. My father worked hard in school. He loved God and the church and his parents. At one time in his life he was going to be a minister, but the hypocrisy of the church bothered him and he became a scientist instead. He has a vision of how science can play the major role in saving the world. This vision puts a light into his eyes. He is a compulsive worker, and I know that he will never stop his work long enough to have a look at some of the things in his life which are blind and tragic. But it's not my business to print. About me and my father I don't know. I keep thinking of how hard it was for him to say anything nice about me to my face. Maybe he favored me and felt guilty about it, but he couldn't say anything nice. A lot of times I thought he would break my heart. Once he complimented me for something I was wearing. "You ought to wear that kind of thing more often," he said, and I looked into the mirror and I was wearing a black dress which I hated. I was fourteen then and I remember thinking, "Hah. I remind him of his mother in this thing."

My father is the saint of the family. You work at something until you exhaust yourself, so that you can be good at it, and with it you try to improve the lot of the sad ones, the hungry ones, the sick ones. You raise your children trying to teach them decency and respect for human life. Once when I was about thirteen he asked me if I would accept a large sum of money for the death of a man who was going to die anyway. I didn't quite understand. If I was off the hook, and just standing by, and then the man was killed by someone else, why shouldn't I take a couple of million? I told him sure, I'd take the money, and he laughed his head off. "That's immoral," he said. I didn't know what immoral meant, but I knew something was definitely wrong taking money for a man's life.

Once in my life I spent a month alone with my father. In 1950, when he was assigned to a project in Baghdad, Iraq, for UNESCO, my sisters got jaundice, and couldn't leave the States. My father left on schedule, for a month of briefing in Paris before going to Baghdad. I had jaundice too, but I didn't tell anyone. I wanted very badly to go to Paris. So despite bad pains in my stomach and black urine which I flushed in a hurry so he wouldn't see, and a general yellow hue which was creeping over my skin, and sometimes seemed to be tinting everything I looked at, I took full advantage of that time with my old man in Gay Paree. We bicycled everywhere, and bought long fresh bread and cheese and milk. We sat in outdoor cafés and had tea, and while he was busy at UNESCO house, I would run the elevators and visit secretaries and draw pictures of everyone and go off to feed pigeons in the park. Neither of us spoke French, but we faked it. One night in a restaurant, we couldn't understand anything on the dessert menu, so my father took a gamble and said, "Ça, s'il vous plaît," pointing to the word "Confiture," and they brought him a dish of strawberry jam, which he ate.

Once the family was together in Baghdad, I developed a terrible fear that my father was going to die. The fact is he almost killed himself tampering with the stupid brick oven which had to be lit in order to get hot bath water. He was "experimenting" with it—trying to determine how fast he could get the fire going by increasing the flow of kerosene into the oven. It exploded in his face, setting his clothes on fire and giving him third degree burns on his hands and face. He covered his eyes instinctively, or he would probably have been blinded, but his eyelashes and eyebrows were burned off anyway. Pauline passed out after telling Mother that "Popsy is on fire," and Mother wrapped him up in a sheet and called the English hospital for an ambulance. While we waited for the ambulance, my father tapped his feet in rhythm on the kitchen tiles, and cleared his throat every four or five seconds. He smelled terrible, and except for Mother, we just stood there. I was probably praying. Mother took me to the hospital to see him once, and I felt bad because I got dizzy when I saw his hands. They had big pussy blisters on them, and his face looked like a Rice Krispie, and I wanted to make him feel better, but I also wanted to go stick my head out the window and get some fresh air. When he came home from the hospital he was bandaged so that all you could see were his eyes and his ears. He held classes for his students at home. He is a brilliant teacher, and they loved him. I know they loved him, because the room smelled so awful from burnt flesh and Middle East medication that I felt sick every time I passed his door. And they came every day to learn and to see him.

My father teaches physics. He is a Ph.D. in physics, and we all wish he'd had just one boy who wasn't so opposed to school, to degrees, to formal education of any kind. One child to show some interest when he does physics experiments at the dinner table. But then it must be partly because we felt obligated to be student-types that we have all rebelled so completely. I can barely read. That is to say, I

51

would rather do a thousand things before sitting down to read.

He used to tell us we should read the dictionary. He said it was fun and very educational. I've never gotten into it.

When we lived in Clarence Center, New York (it was a town of eight hundred people, and as far as they knew, we were niggers; Mother says that someone yelled out the window to me, "Hey, nigger!" and I said, "You ought to see me in the summertime!"), my father had a job working in Buffalo. It was some kind of armaments work. I just knew that it was secret, or part of it was secret, and that we began to get new things like a vacuum cleaner, a refrigerator, a fancy coffee pot, and one day my father came home with a little Crosley car. We were so excited about it that we drove it all over the front lawn, around the trees and through the piles of leaves. He was driving, Mother was in the front seat, and we three kids were in the back. The neighbors knew we were odd to begin with, but this confirmed it. Mother was embarrassed and she kept clutching my father's arm and saying, "Oh, Abo!" but he would take a quick corner around a tree and we'd all scream with laughter and Mother gave up and had hysterics.

Then something started my father going to Quaker meetings. We all had to go. It meant we had to sit and squelch giggles for about twenty minutes, and then go off with some kind old lady who planted each of us a bean in a tin can, and told us it was a miracle that it would push its little head up above the damp earth and grow into a plant. We knew it was a miracle, and we knew she was kind, but we made terrible fun of her the entire time and felt guilty about it afterwards.

While we were in the side room with the kind old lady, watching our beans perform miracles, my father was in the grown-up room, the room where they observe silence for a whole hour, and he was having a fight with his conscience. It took him less than a year of those confrontations with himself in that once a week silence to realize that he would have to give up either the silences or his job. Next thing I knew we were packing up and moving across the country. My father had taken a job as a professor of physics at the University of Redlands for about one-half the pay, and one-tenth the prestige—against the advice of everyone he knew except my mother. Since leaving Buffalo in 1947, he's never accepted a job that had anything to do with armaments, offense, defense, or whatever they prefer to call it. Last night I had a dream about him. I dreamed he was sitting next to himself in a theater. One of him was as he is now, and the other was the man of thirty years ago. I kept trying to get him to look at himself and say hello. Both faces smiled very understandingly, but neither would turn to greet the other.

I don't think he's ever understood me very well. He's never understood my compulsiveness, my brashness, my neuroses, my fears, my antinationalism (though he's changing on that), my sex habits, my loose way of handling money. I think often I startle him, and many times I please him. Sometimes I have put him through hell, like when I decided to live with Michael when I was twenty. "You mean you're going to . . . *live* with him?" "Yes," I said, and my father took a sleeping bag and went to the beach for two days, because Michael was staying in the house. Years later he sent me an article by Bertrand Russell, whom he respects very much, underlining the part which said that if young people could have a chance at "experimental marriages" while they were in college, they might know more about what it's all about before they actually got married. My father wrote that it always amazed him how I came to conclusions intuitively which took him years to realize.

At one time, my father couldn't stand to have a bottle of wine in the house. Whenever my aunt on my mother's side came to visit us in Cambridge, Mother would buy a bottle of wine, and she and my aunt would have a glass of wine before dinner. Sometimes my sisters and I took a glass, too, though I think Pauline was the only one who ever actually drank it down. One time, after my aunt had left, Father called a pow-wow, and we all gathered in the kitchen. Father's forehead was crumpled and overcast. He cleared his throat about a hundred times and made some vague opening statements about this generation and how we were still kids, and how he didn't really know how to deal with the problem at hand. Mother finally asked him what he was talking about, and he said, "Well, if any of my kids turns out to be an alcoholic, I'll know where it started. Right here in my own home." We looked at Mother to feel out the appropriate reaction, and she tried to be serious but couldn't be so we got into a half humorous argument with Father. I told him he was lucky because none of us was at all interested in booze, and most of our friends got crocked every weekend, if not more often, and he said where were our standards, that his father would have had to leave home if he'd ever so much as tasted alcohol. It was all so entirely ridiculous that we ladies had to check ourselves to keep from making too much fun, or his feelings would be hurt, and he would get really angry. A few years later, my mother and father moved to Paris, and he learned to drink, and I think even to enjoy, wine with dinner. Knowing the way I am, it's amazing that my father's puritanism about liquor did not set me up nicely for dipsomania, but for some reason, I have a total dislike for alcohol. And for cigarettes. And for the more recent fads: I don't smoke marijuana, or, needless to say, use any other drugs. I get high as a cloud on one sleeping pill, if that's what it means to get high, and it's not a whole lot different from what I feel like on a fall day in New England, or listening to the Faure Requiem, or dancing to soul music or singing in a Mississippi church.

About him and money. I guess he had to be conscious of budgets and things while he was bringing us up. I remember hearing the word "budget" all the time, and seeing Mother take dollar bills out of separate pockets in a little brown envelope which folded like an accordion. I never understood why, if there was five dollars in "food" she couldn't switch it over to "movies." I think sometimes she did. But my old man has plenty of money now. He's worked compulsively ever since I can remember. Now that he has a certain amount of wealth, I think he likes it, even though he may not be able, really, to accept it. He buys tons of life insurance. And things like encyclopedias and science journals. I remember the first time I really made any money: I came home to Cambridge from Chicago, where I'd had my first and only job singing in a nightclub. I had made four hundreds dollars in two weeks, and I carried it all home in cash—mostly twenties. I walked in the front door and put down my suitcase, ripped the four hundred out of my purse and threw it into the air and yelled, "Up for grabs!" as it fluttered around me to the living room floor. I probably gave everyone some, because I remember feeling bad for having all of it, and I didn't realize until much later that the incident upset him—perhaps only because I could earn four hundred dollars in two weeks, without having had to study for it. But I don't know. Just before I made that money singing, I had the only legitimate job I've ever had outside of singing (which I've always felt was cheating). I taught people how to drive Vespa motor scooters, and took them for their license when they'd learned. My father let me use his old beat-up

Vespa to get to work, though I know he liked using it himself. I was paid a dollar and a quarter an hour for the most hair-raising job on the payroll, and eventually I quit because, a) I was going crazy from people who had no sense of balance, and b) I was offered the job singing in the nightclub. But I saved enough money from dragging people into the store to buy motor scooters and making 20 percent on the sale, to buy a new scooter, one with mirrors and four speeds and rubber footmats and a book carrier, and I drove it home, dizzy with delight, and presented it to my father as a gift. I recall a strange, stilted response when I told him it was for him. There was some wisecrack about money. Mother told me later that she went into the bathroom and cried, but I think I was so pleased about my gift that I wasn't really put off. I had never thought that it might hurt my father's pride to receive something from his child which was, by our standards, expensive. He must have been pleased too, though, because he drove it all the time. Sometimes I think he has a double reaction to everything I do.

The major part of my childhood was spent in fighting off terror of things which don't exist, and I don't think my father ever understood that kind of fear. The overriding and most terrifying bogeyman of my life, which has been with me since my earliest memories, and remains faithfully with me though now it seldom puts me out of commission, has been a fear of vomiting. It has used up and wasted and blackened many hours of my life. But my father never had a notion of what I was talking about when I cried and shook and said, "You know . . . It's that thing again . . ." While I was in junior high school and even high school, I was still going to my parents' bedroom, sometimes five nights a week, and climbing in their bed, all hot and cold and shaking, pleading for Mother to say the key sentences which would begin to send the fear away. Always I felt dreadfully ill. Always I wanted to hear only one thing: "You won't be sick." Always I kept my food down, though the nausea was so extreme that anyone in his right mind would have stuck his finger down his throat and been done with it. My father would follow Mother and me to the bathroom in the middle of the night, and as I sat on the toilet clutching their hands, he would pat my head and say things to Mother like, "Did she eat something funny?" or, "S'pose she's got a little bug?" and Mother would shake her head and signal him that he was saying the wrong thing again. Once, as I was crawling into bed crying, and Mother was moving over to give me room, mumbling to me that everything would be all right, my father half woke up and said to Mother in a soft voice which had shades of annoyance, "What's the matter with her? Is it her stomach?" I think I said, "No, it's my head," and the degree to which my anger rose equaled the degree to which the nausea sank. One time my mother was out of the house, and I had a bad attack of whatever you would call that terror, and I had no one to call but my father. I was crying, and I told him what to say. "Just tell me I won't throw up. You know I won't, so just tell me I don't have to."

"What's so bad about throwing up?" he asked. Those perfectly reasonable words threw me into a fresh panic and I let go of his arm and covered my ears and sobbed and said, "No, no, don't say that, you can't say that . . ."

"Look," he said, "right now there must be a hundred sick Arabs throwing up this very minute. It's nothing. You just, blughh, and it's over, and then you feel great . . ." That was advice I was in no way ready to hear, and I simply hated him for it. He has to admit now that the doctors I've seen over the past ten years have been a great help to me. But his general feeling is that psychiatry is for the rich, and one could rise above time-consuming phobias (which, I'm convinced, are as foreign to him as the joy of physics is to me) and carry on in a healthy manner if one only had enough to do. In a sense I agree with him. Part of the fact that my fears play a minor role in my life now is that I have so many passions and commitments that terror is replaced and pushed aside. But no one can force constructive activity upon a child who is, above all things, paralyzed with fear. The network of short circuits and crossed wires that forced my father and me to play in such a way upon each other's weaknesses was, and probably still is, more entangled than either of us would like to admit. We have reduced the entire situation, which is more than partially solved, to his accepting the fact that psychiatry has helped me, and my accepting his jokes about psychiatry; and neither of us ever gives the other so much as a peek at what has gone on between us for the last twenty-six years, and what goes on still. Perhaps it's easier this way.

Lately my father has told me, off and on, that he is 100 percent behind me in the things I do. I think that's hard for him to say, for lots of reasons, one being the reason I mentioned earlier—that he has trouble telling me nice things about myself or what I do. Another is that he hasn't always gone along with my radical ideas of nonviolence and antinationalism, or my feelings that formal education is meaningless at best, and that universities are baby-sitting operations. Even though he was peace-marching long before I was, when I swung, I swung all the way, and left my father looking and acting, in my opinion, fairly moderate. But he has changed very much in the last five years, and I know that when my mother and Mimi and I went to jail for doing Civil Disobedience at the Army induction center, he had no doubts that we were doing the right thing, and he took over the Institute for Non-Violence for the weekend seminars. I think that all the while he was working with UNESCO in Paris, traveling around the world, trying to help find ways of teaching science in underdeveloped countries, he was more concerned than he admitted to himself about two problems: One was how he could teach people the wonders of science and at the same time keep them from simply trying to ape the powerful nations of the world and race to discover new scientific ways to destroy themselves and each other. The temptation for power is so great, and unfortunately, what power has always meant is one's ability and efficiency to murder one's neighbor. The other problem that haunted my father had to do with UNESCO itself: It was filled with power-hungry and money-hungry individuals, and he never wanted to admit it. My mother told me of a time when they were at a dinner party of UNESCO science division men and their wives. Some of the men were loosening up on wine and my father was talking about his difficulties in South America. His colleagues were not really interested in his successes or failures in teaching science to Brazilians, and that fact became more and more apparent. Finally, one of them said something to the effect of, "Aw c'mon, Baez, you don't really give a damn about science teaching methods, do you?" My mother was completely floored by this, and she said, "That's what we're here for," and asked the man why *he* was with UNESCO. He had a publishing job, the man said, and it hadn't really paid much: UNESCO paid a hell of a lot more, plus you got to travel, so he had gone to work for UNESCO and ended up in Paris. Not a bad deal all the way around. He went on kidding my father, who was struck dumb; and Mother did something she doesn't do unless she's in a state of shock or fury—she gave something resembling a speech. "My husband was an idealist when he came to work for UNESCO.

61

He's a pacifist. He's concerned about the fact that people are starving to death and he thought the best way he could help out would be through UNESCO, to spread the uses of science to people who need it. Maybe we're just crazy, but I never imagined anyone came to work here for any other reason."

While he was with UNESCO, he seemed to lose his sense of humor. When I would visit them in Paris, sometimes it seemed that all I ever heard him say was, "I have this deadline . . . You know I just have to keep to this schedule . . ." He was trying to finish a book, which took him eight years to write. A basic text in physics. I seriously thought he would not ever complete that book, that it was like an eternally incomplete project he had to have to keep himself worn out. And I thought he was afraid to get it printed. But it was published while he was still in Paris. It's beautiful. The introduction is preceded by a picture of a huge rock suspended over the ocean. The picture makes you want to sit down heavily on the floor, or throw a paperweight out the window and watch it hit the sidewalk. There are little bits of human philosophy preceding each chapter, over eight hundred pictures, and the book is dedicated to "my wife, Joan, and my three daughters, Pauline, Joanie, and Mimi." And on page 274 there is a drawing which illustrates how an image is projected onto a television screen, and the image being projected is of a familiar-looking girl with long black hair, who stands holding a guitar.

In my estimation, my old man got his sense of humor back when he left Paris, and returned to the States. Toward the end of a course he was teaching at Harvard, a crash summer course, based on his book, he gave what he later described to me as the "demonstration of the century." He told the class that he was going to give an example of jet propulsion. He had a little red wagon brought in, and then he took the fire extinguisher off the wall and sat down in the wagon and jet propelled himself in circles around the front of the room, explaining, at the top of his voice, exactly what was happening technically. The students stood on their chairs and gave him an ovation, and it was all so overwhelming that he repeated the experiment. He shouted halfway through it for someone to open the door, and shot himself out into the hall, and disappeared. When he came back the bell had rung and the class was still there, cheering.

Right now, in 1967, my mother has planted my father and herself in a beautiful place in Carmel Valley, about one mile from my house, and not far from Pauline. A while after they began to be settled, I asked him if he could give himself permission to enjoy the luxury of his new home, his swimming pool, the endless beauty of the hills around. He tried to avoid my question by making a joke, but I said I was serious. We were sitting on the floor on a nice carpet, and he smoothed his hands over it as he leaned back against the wall. He looked very brown and Mexican in that moment, and I

63

watched his profile against the valley hills as he struggled with himself. He said something about other people in the world, and about hunger. Then he looked up and gave me a smile of such a combination of things. "Yes, honey," he said, "I think I can enjoy it . . . if I keep myself busy enough . . ."

MORNING DEVILS

Some of the past creeps up on me: cold metal green lockers, and the girls' gym volleyball court, the cold nurse's room and the ice-cold nurse, and the warm safety of the school cot and blanket.

Tenth grade and I am still fighting my sunless morning devils. Ice forms in my bones and something vile erupts in my stomach. The kids' faces become animated familiarity and the noise is unbearable. I'm freezing. If I stop walking, I'll feel how dizzy I am. Please. Get out of my way. You don't understand. No books. No binders. No questions, no quizzes, no tiptoeing around the library, because I am on a different planet, and not a single one of you understands. I want to go home. I'll go to the nurse's room.

"Got your period, dear?"

"I have to lie down."

"Are you ill?"

"I'll be all right after a while. If I can lie down."

"Do you have a fever?"

"No. It's just something that happened to me. If I can sleep it will probably go away."

"Well, gosh . . . I don't think that sounds like much of a reason to be out of class . . ."

She changes her mind when she looks at me. I'm shaking all over like a skinny kid who's been in a pool until his mouth has turned purple and he can't hold his Coke without spilling. She gives me a bed and a blanket. I'll keep my legs moving, my hands rubbing together in some pattern, and my mind is racing in spirals around the center of fright. Each time I reach the narrowing bottom of the spiral something almost automatically throws me back to the rim like a pinball, and then, as if by gravitational force, I begin the downward whirl again. There are other girls in the room. That's a help. Their voices drone. My hands are warming up. I scrunch down and warm my feet with my hands. The shaking has stopped. I'll listen to the girls for a while.

They are two society girls. They set it up the day before to have phony cramps and skip a test they know they will both flunk and go to the nurse's room to jabber about someone they both hate. They talk in animated whispers.

My God, they are cruel.

I am no threat to them.

How nice it would be to be a threat. If I were the one they were concerned about, all the flaws they were whispering about would be mine and would mean nothing to me. Their silly gossip would just be part of the game that would make me their equal. Their pretty, painted, eggshell equal. And when I came into the nurse's room they would have shushed and started fingering their Saint Christophers. Then, with big "Hi's" they would have called me over, and drummed up fake secrets that included me. And I would have been their pal and we'd have talked about someone else until the bell rang.

The room is cold, but I am warm under the school blanket. There is an unformed thought in my head. Without my being aware of it, someone has placed a portrait of calm just in front of the spiral, and the spiral is fading into the distance, as though I were driving away from a ghastly carnival. I turn my head on the pillow and move my hand up to my face, following up a sudden desire to inspect my nails. I look at my hands. I know my hands are beautiful. They are very special. At dusk, when the dimming sky compliments everything and makes it either glow, or fade and look dreamlike, I watch my hands. The nails and the webbed part at the base of my fingers jump out at me like platinum on brown velvet, and I know that these are the hands of an Indian princess. Sometimes I put a gold ring on the longest toe of my foot, and it glows against the dusty ground. My hair is soft and black and it shines blue when it is just washed.

I glance over at the girls. I feel unworried,

and I smile at them. They smile back in a funny way, and as I turn away I wonder if I didn't count to them when I smiled like that. I wonder if I like them. I wonder if they like me . . .

But the portrait of calm has moved in on me, and the blessed drowsiness has slowed my thoughts into daydreams, and the daydreams are floating me off into dreams . . . I will sleep away all the sunless ghouls and tiring fears . . . I will float when the two girls recover from their cramps and get nurse's slips back to class. I will sleep an anxious sleep during the bell-clanging racket of class change, when the nurse might come in and wake me up . . . but she has forgotten, or remembered that she never knows what to say to me, so today I can stay. I will sleep an exhausted sleep. I will dream a multitude of happy summers, and wake up in harmony with the noon of day, ready for the sun.

DREAM

On a train in some other country, I don't know which, there was a woman sitting with a twelve-year-old boy. The boy was trying to kiss her, and it was kind of nice, because she was letting him. He was trying to be her lover, from stuff he'd seen, and at one point he buried his face in her hair and kissed her neck, and then licked her face and said, "That's how they fuck." She was pleased and happy.

IRA

I met Ira when I was sixteen. My father was still taking us to Quaker meetings. We all hated it, but it never occurred to me not to go, because it was too much of a struggle contending with my father's hurt feelings and the ensuing family disasters. Anyway, there I was, sixteen, squirming through the Sunday morning silences and occasionally teaching the kindergarten class. They call it "first-day school."

One sunny but boring Sunday, as I recall now, there was a funny bearded man at the meetinghouse, and he had a laugh like a goat. He smiled and laughed lots, and his eyes were always filling with tears. He was some kind of legendary person, because most of the kids already knew him. I heard he was going to take over our high school first-day classes. That's all I can remember about the first time I met Ira—

that it was sunny, and that he had a laugh like a goat.

He did take our class, and we began to call his sessions the "sermons on the pavement." He talked a lot about Gandhi, and something called nonviolence, and we read from a book by a Chinese philosopher named Lao-tse. One of the things Lao-tse said was, "The is is the was of what shall be," and I thought that that was the cleverest thing I'd ever heard.

I began to grow very fond of the bearded guru with the goat laugh. I felt he might have answers that no one else had. I asked him how I could learn to get along with my sister Mimi. She was twelve then, and very beautiful, and we fought all the time. Not in a big way, but by nasty little put-downs and ugly faces, and once in a while nail marks left in each other's arms. It seemed so endless and unkind. Ira said to pretend that it was the last hour of her life, as, he pointed out, it might well be. So I tried out his plan. Mimi reacted strangely at first, the way anyone does when a blueprint is switched on him without his being consulted. I learned to look at her, and as a result, to see her for the first time. I began to love her. The whole process took about one summer. It's curious, but there is perhaps no one in the world as dear to me as Mimi.

Ira dressed in corduroys and sweatshirts and a baggy duffle coat and a beat-up alpine hat. He began to come by my house on his bicycle every morning before school. I'd skip first period and he'd be late to work, and we'd walk in the morning sun and make jokes about the world, and at the same time I knew that he and I felt desperately that we must do something to try and help the world. My father once asked Ira what he saw in this sixteen-year-old, to visit me every morning. Ira just told him that I was extraordinary.

I began accompanying Ira to places when he spoke. I heard more things about Gandhi and love and nonviolence and a brotherhood of man, which he said didn't exist yet. Once we went to a Jewish junior high school summer camp. Ira spoke, and I sang, and he made some remark to the effect that we would have to travel around doing that someday, and maybe we could make a change in the world.

One day I asked Ira to visit my school, Palo Alto High School. He came to an English class with me, and the teacher was late, so Ira got up and began to answer questions. When the teacher arrived we were talking about life and war and love and nonviolence, and the teacher had the good sense to let us continue. But the administration had heard by now that English 12 had let an agitator loose in front of the kiddies, and Ira and I were called to the front office at the end of the period. The vice-principal waited until the bell had rung for the next class, and then he began to explain to Ira how it was illegal for him to be on the campus without a certain pink pass signed by the principal. I asked him if he could please give us one, and he said no he could not, that it had to be applied for by one of the students, and then decided upon by the administration, and would I please go to my class now. I asked him why I should go to my class, and he said because the bell had rung. I said I was staying until my guest left, and the vice-principal said no, no, go back to class, how could I learn anything if I didn't go to class. I told him I was learning something right that minute. I was learning how he and Ira acted with each other. He gave up and just tried to hurry Ira out the door. I took Ira's arm and walked him out of the office and down the hall to the front entrance. I knew the vice-principal was peeking from somewhere so I walked out of the building onto the porch, just to give him a scare, and I shook Ira's hand good-bye. I don't know why I didn't keep walking. It would have been right. The only real teacher at school that day was being kicked off the campus.

Once we went to Dinah's Shack together for dinner. I went barefoot, and he in his regular funny outfit. Dinah's Shack has a smorgasbord, with lots of salads and cheeses, which Ira liked, because he didn't eat meat. I ordered a piece of roast beef and then couldn't eat it. I just ate things off the smorgasbord table. We walked home after dinner, right down about three miles of main highway, and then across the Stanford hayfields, talking and laughing—an intellectual hobo and a gloriously deteriorating remnant of the American public school system. In the middle of the fields I noticed that it seemed that the clouds were moving with us. Ira says that I stopped and said, with great relief, that I was glad my father wasn't there, because he would have had to explain it.

When I went East, at the end of my senior year, I wrote Ira only now and then. He was by then, and remains still such a constant thing to me that it doesn't matter if he is nearby, or in some other state: I knew he was a part of my fate, and it didn't alarm me to sense that.

On my first trip home, after a year in the East, I went straight to see Ira. No one was home at his house, so I sat down in the living room and waited. A car pulled up and I ran out to see. It was Ira's wife. "Hi!" I yelled, and ran to greet her. We met at the mailbox, and I tried to give her a hug, but she was fishing around with the mail, and she said "shit" under her breath.

"Bad letter?" I said, moving away a little, giving her room for bad humor.

"Not exactly," she replied. I figured out that it was not the mail, but me, and I asked her if she wanted me to leave. She said no, so I stayed and helped her clean the house. She began to talk. She said Ira was a pain in the ass and all these women thought he was a saint. Did I think he was a saint? No, I said. She went on to say that he was so far from being a saint that it wasn't funny. He was impossible to live with, didn't take proper care of the children, went off to all these damn meetings, and all these damn women kept coming by the house asking for him. I asked her why she didn't leave him, and I don't remember what she said. Ira came home and she drove off in a rage, and that was the first time I'd seen Ira get angry. He said she was a moron, and I said I thought she was kind of nice, but that we would probably never hit it off.

His kids are great. The boy was about eight when I first saw him. He was shy and hostile and had extravagantly large eyes and long eye-lashes. He was always beating up on Ira, and wanting to play guns and war games and begging Ira to get a TV so he could watch the Westerns. It was partly to tease his pacifist father, and partly open anger. Ira refused to get a TV so Mark watched it at the neighbor's house and told Ira all about it later on when there were guests in the house. Ira and Mark and I had dinner together once when he was about ten. I remember that he had a great sense of humor, and that he made terrible wise-cracks to me about Ira, and terrible wisecracks to Ira about his mother.

When Mark was eight, Nicole was ten. She was beautiful, very messy and wild looking, very intelligent, and fond of nature. She kept a pet frog. Once, when she was six she saw a truckload of chickens going to be slaughtered, and she didn't eat meat for a year. Ira tells me of another time when she was about eleven, she came into his study late at night where he sat reading. He said, "Hi, darling."

"Did Gandhi have a penis?" she asked.

"Yes," he answered.

"Did he have a vagina too?"

"No," said Ira. "He was a man, and men just have a penis."

"Oh," she said, and turned to leave the study.

"What made you ask that?" Ira said.

"Well," she said, pausing in the doorway, "it's just that he was so nice . . . I thought he might have had both."

She and her brother had always called their father Ira until he and his wife got a divorce, and then she called him "Daddy Dumpling."

Ira was born into an affluent family in St. Louis, Missouri. His father was a surgeon. The Sandperls had a home in St. Louis and an apartment in the Plaza Hotel in New York. The images I have from what he's told me of his childhood suggest something equivalent to the story-book heroine, Eloise. There was a maid and a butler who doubled as chauffeur. Ira says he was able to escape from that mold because of his mother. "We were a good Jewish family," he says. "We were allowed to do just about anything but be stupid. We could *not* be stupid. My mother thought violence was the stupidest thing of all, so I was really a pacifist from a very early age." As a very young man, he was sensitive and wise, gentle, clever, bright, and extremely stubborn. He had the face of a young Indian prince, and an ego to match—all with the added attraction of his limp which came from a case of polio he contracted shortly after he was born. When he went away to Stanford, he sent his shirts home to St. Louis to be laundered, because he couldn't find a laundry on campus that came up to snuff. He dressed in Brooks Brothers clothes, and had affairs with very attractive, usually married women.

76

Then one day he walked past a bookstore and saw, in the window, a picture of a skinny brown man in a loincloth, sitting at a spinning wheel. Ira had no money with him at the time, but said he would come back and pay for the book the next day if the clerk would let him take it home. The clerk said that anyone interested in that book was not likely to be dishonest, and he gave Ira the book.

"Gandhi, the rat!" says Ira. "He ruined my life!"

Ira fell in love with nonviolence and dropped out of Stanford in order to pursue his education.

Ira is a rascal who longs to be a saint. He is lured by the life of the recluse, by monks' robes and silent hillsides and the nonexistent waters of purification. He longs to be free of earthly ties and desires. He meditates all the time, and carries on what he calls his monologue with God, and then loses his temper in public and chastises himself for hours afterwards, putting his hat over his face and groaning to me, "Oh God, I was awful. Just awful. I'll never make it."

"You're right, Ira," I'll answer. "We're both going to die and go to hell. If we have another life we'll be snails."

"I just want to be free of all desire. That's all I ask," Ira says, waving his hat in the air, and returning to our ancient theme.

"Why didn't you say so? I've got these five simple steps right here in my pocket . . ."

"You," he says. "You're a worse rat than I."

"Oh no. I'm just as bad in the things I do, but I don't lie about them afterwards the way you do . . ."

"Oh God, you're a wretch . . ." he says, sinking low in his chair, and we laugh. And we both know that we lack real humility, and we wish we were like Socrates, who *knew* that he knew nothing. Our minds are cluttered, and some nights we need Seconal to get to sleep. We know we get lonesome in our boredom with ourselves and have to call out for help.

"On my lonesome road to God I need no earthly companions," said Gandhi. And he spent his life trying to meet God, as he said, face to face. That's what I would like to do. And that's what Ira would like to do. We feel, like Gandhi, that God cannot be found anywhere but in total involvement with humankind. It was Ira who suggested to me that the only truth he really knew was that no one knew the Truth, and therefore no one had a right to take another man's life for his idea of Truth. He says that we will never be perfect, but must constantly attempt to approximate being kind, decent, thoughtful. He introduced me to the line of T. S. Eliot: "For us there is only the trying. The rest is not our business." And I know that he tries.

I have heard him say a thousand times that the only way to peace is through peaceful means; that a peaceful end would not justify wicked means; that in fact wicked means have only brought about a continuation of wickedness; that the only way to peace is through nonviolent political action.

"When will men learn to stop being so stupid?" Over and over he's asked me that. Over and over he's said, "Nonviolence means changing the assumption that it is OK to kill, and working from that point to create political, economical, social, institutional, psychological alternatives to war." Or, "Nationalism is nothing more than a primitive attachment to land—something we must grow out of if we are to survive this century." Or, "Every time I see a child I remember what I'm fighting for. No one has the right to kill children." And then: "It's a strange and glorious life, Beazle," he will say, "and I feel just terribly lucky to be alive."

Ira's passions are nonviolence and literature. He buys about fifteen books a week, reads them all, and retains anything which can be of use in his nonviolent arsenal. His living room is a library, with a section of books reserved for Gandhi. When he reads, he lies on his back with his knees up and his head up, sometimes cupping one hand around the back of his neck.

When we are at home in Carmel Valley we run the Institute for Non-Violence together, speak locally as much as we can, eat dinner at a Mexican restaurant called Plaza Linda, and go to the movies. We like spy movies and second-rate Westerns.

But we are not at home much of the time. Singing and speaking tours keep us running. Usually wherever I am giving a concert, Ira will meet with any or all of the peace people he can find in the area. I love being on the road with him. He comes to my hotel room for breakfast and over two beers and a cigar, tells me the news of the day. Ira is back in Brooks Brothers suits now, and we both have a weakness for really good hotels. He is always backstage when I sing, available when I cave in and panic. "You get to cave in," he says, when I curl up in the dressing room, in tiresome familiar tears, with my head in his lap. "You get to cave in like everybody else," he says. And I do.

So we travel together, teach together, march together, laugh and cry together, sit-in together, and go to jail together. He is an endless joy to me.

Contrary to all outward appearances, Ira and I have never been in love with each other in the conventional sense, and have never had an affair. It has been a spiritual marriage which has brought only the most constructive and tender companionship. One night, during the year of Ira's second marriage, as we sat in the lamp-lit restaurant of some fine hotel in some foreign land, Ira with his Bloody Mary and I with my tomato juice, we had a little exchange of true confessions on why neither of us had ever had the desire to go to bed with the other. I guess we'd never brought it up before because we each felt we would injure the other's ego. We decided that to have had an affair would have been much too dangerous. Neither of us can stand to be on the losing end of anything, and we are both, by nature, hopelessly inconsistent, or, more bluntly, fickle. We decided that a safety valve in each of us decided that *that* was the one person to beware of, and the danger of an imminent fall of pride warded off any sexual attraction. How grateful we both are, because we seem very bad at mixing sex with love over any period of time, and, the nonviolent movement being what it is today—namely, practically nonexistent—would have suffered greatly from the disintegration of one of its most active teams. But nonviolence is stuck with us, and we are stuck with nonviolence. And it's a glorious life, Ira, and I feel terribly lucky to know you.

DREAM

Dreamed we all went to work for some evil man. He ran a super-James Bond efficient resort-like science grounds, where he smuggled very expensive stuff and used the hell out of people. Popsy thought it was an advanced science study center, so the family moved there. The director had rules like the ones in the prison. I was playing with a little girl, and we were running on the grass. I saw that they were paving over the grass with oil and gravel, and I was disappointed, because the grass was so pretty. When the child's mother arrived (she was a new employee), I told her the child would get all sticky from the tar, and just then a lady guard approached and said something like "silence rules," which meant that the lady had to act as if she didn't see me. Couldn't speak to me or recognize me. She didn't take it too seriously, so I knew she wouldn't last long there . . . At one point I was eating a piece of cake, taking the crumbly part out of the frosting and throwing the frosting away, and leaning over a wastebasket, and another lady employee stopped her typing and checked up on me with obvious disapproval, and I know she was making a note of my bad behavior . . . There were famous scientists from all over the world, and Popsy was just beginning to settle down and find out his job (he'd been conned into thinking it was wonderful international science work), and Mother and I went off to see a calf get born. The mother cow charged at us, but didn't hurt us. There were always spies in the disguise of scientists wherever we went.

THE WATER LEAVES

Mimi and I were hanging around the Club 47 coffeehouse in Harvard Square. We were on the way home from Newport, '67. We were seeking old friends from eight years before, but also new faces, lots of new faces lined up in the warm New England evening. They let a blind girl in so she could find a seat. I watched the ticket lady hold her hand out timidly to return the change, not wanting to bump the blind girl's hand. When her things were in order the blind girl took the change and began calculating where she would sit, tapping a radar route around the tables and chairs. I went up to her and helped her find a seat.

"This is sort of comfy," I said, showing her the chair. "You're at the back, but on the aisle."

"Thank you very much," she said, sitting

down and folding up her funny collapsible metal cane. Then she faced me and said, "Excuse me, but your voice sounds vaguely familiar . . ."

I told her my name and she let out a squeal.

"I'm Paula. Remember me? From Perkins? Gee, that was eight years ago! Gee, it's good to see you!"

I sat down with her and we chatted. She asked about Mimi, and I called Mimi over. Paula grabbed her cane and purse and jumped up to hug her. Of course, I thought, I had heard stories about the devoted blind kids who had showed up at 47 every time Mimi and Dick were on the bill. Paula fell into an enraptured chat with Mimi, who sat with her head tilted, watching the funny blind girl's face.

"We went to the Winter Festival. It was terrible," she was telling Mimi. "We were in a snowstorm and my eyes were freezing. I thought I would die!"

"Your eyes were freezing?"

"Oh," she said, dropping her head back and facing me, and indicating her eyes by tapping her fingertips around her cheekbones. "These are just shell. See?" I saw two identical clear blue eyes. One of them was sunk a little in the socket.

"You mean glass?" I asked, and then looked closer and saw that her eyes were making almost imperceptible jerking motions in every direction, and that where we have the little dip next to the nose where gnats and sleep settle, Paula had an open place. In that place existed not the miraculous network of an eye, but something more like a dark cavern.

"Yes, they're glass," she said. "When it's really cold they get freezing and press against the socket and it's killing." She showed Mimi her eyes.

"Anyway," she went on, "the Festival was a big bore, except for Pete Seeger, of course." Her face broke into that magnificent odd smile which had never been checked in a mirror.

"Tell me," I said, "what you think of Perkins."

"Well," she said, trying to figure out how I felt about it.

"I was fired from there, myself," I said, to give her free rein. "For sitting on the boys' side, and taking one boy's watch home to be fixed. But it was really because I didn't wear shoes enough of the time, and because I loved the kids. I thought the school was set up for the kids. But it wasn't. It was set up for the teachers and housemothers."

"*You're* not kidding," said Paula in a low voice. "I didn't even know how to go *out* till I left Perkins and took a cane course." She took the folded-up metal off her lap and flipped it into the air and it snapped itself into a cane, as though it were a magic wand.

"Wow!" Mimi and I were impressed. "That's something. Do you like the cane?"

"Oh, I love it. It makes me much more independent than if I had a dog. You know, you're always having to tie the dog to something when you go into a store. This way I'm free to go anywhere I want, whenever I want."

Mimi and I played with the cane for a while.

Perkins Institute for the Blind. Stupid Perkins. Stuffy housemothers and overeducated teachers. Turn out nice clean well-behaved blind types. I wondered how Paula had survived, and then I began remembering the kids. I had worked with the kindergarteners. I was in charge of seven children, twenty hours a day, six days a week. And I lasted for two months.

Little Archie, the problem child, eight operations on his eyes by the age of six, cleft palate, no taste buds or sense of smell, chewed his vitamins up in the morning, dropped his glass eye in the oatmeal and cried in noisy sorrow that he'd lost his eye . . . I felt sick trying to wash his face the first day, because both his eye sockets were infected and oozing . . . so at the breakfast table I couldn't eat, and when the head housemother said, "Is something wrong?" I said, "Archie's face, it's sort of icky . . ." and began to cry.

"Oh goodness, dear, we can't let a little thing like that get us down," she said brightly, and she took Archie off to wash his face and threw up her breakfast.

Archie's mother was always the first parent to drop him at the school on Sunday afternoons and the last to pick him up on Fridays, and the housemothers didn't give a damn about him in between because he was a bad boy and all the operations had made him hard to look at. I begged the women to quit calling him a bad boy, and said I would spend extra time with him. It turned out that Archie didn't know how to hug. So every time he came around I'd grab all the children I could find and be hugging them when he got near. He had a tiny bit of vision in his one eye if he poked it with his fist, and he'd climb up over the kids to find out what was happening. I'd be saying, "Oh Gail, what a lovely hug, thank you!" and so Archie, with one fist jammed into his good eye, was beginning to see that he'd been missing something that looked like fun. And then one night after I'd put him to bed, and we'd said the horrible little Perkins prayer, I gave Archie a kiss on the forehead and said good-night, and as I got up to go he said, "Hey, Miss Joan, don't I get a hug?" and after we'd had a big warm hug there was a fiendish smile on his funny cockeyed face on the pillow, and he said, "You know what, Miss Joan? You're a good kid."

There was odd Lila, who had had polio and thought that she still couldn't raise her arms. She held her elbows close to her sides and rolled her poor head around day and night, and was bald in spots and matty haired at the back of her skull. She screamed in her sleep, wet her bed, and pretended she couldn't speak. The truth was that no one knew how much she could hear or say, because she wouldn't respond to testing, or teasing, or just plain loud noises. Still, every night when we had songs, I would sing "Takes a Worried Man to Sing a Worried Song," substituting, in every chorus, the name of each child in place of the word "man," and every night I would watch carefully when I sang Lila's name, and she would just roll her head and bang her fists together. One afternoon I was carrying her around in my arms, chatting to her as if she could hear, and I noticed that she was smiling, something she never did. Suddenly, in perfect rhythm and perfect tune, she sang softly, "Takes a worried Lila, to sing a worried song, Takes a worried Lila, to sing a worried song . . ." I didn't say anything to her, I just walked fast to where the head housemother was, and pointed very subtly at Lila.

"I'm worried now, but I won't be worried long," sang Lila, finishing up the verse just as the housemother was taking in her breath to say, "Oh, and who do we have here?" and leaning over to wipe off the lunch table. But by the time she had stopped bustling and had stood up to give us her attention, Lila had stopped singing and was smiling a viciously happy smile.

"Never mind," I said, and the housemother never-minded.

I walked off and jiggled Lila up and down a few times.

"So we goofed, huh, Lila?" I said, but Lila had stopped smiling and gone back to rolling her head, and in the time I was at Perkins, I never heard her sing or speak again.

Ming Lo was flown in from Chicago. He didn't walk. He spun in circles down the school hall. He knew two words, "Aunty" and "eat." If he was left alone for more than thirty seconds at night he would call out, in the most heart-breaking voice, "Aunty! Aunty!" So for a while we took night shifts holding Ming's hand, so that he could go to sleep and get some relief from the new unfamiliar hell into which some-one had dropped him.

Ming was a compulsive eater, bed-wetter, and stripper, and as he grew used to the new life with all his Caucasian aunties, he felt free to slip out of his bed at nap time, spin out into the hall, strip all his clothes off, do pee-pee on the floor, and lie down in it, like a great fat Buddha gone mad, not just smiling, but laugh-ing until he hurt. I always hoped to find him first, because the women slapped his hand and said, "Dirty Ming," and chalked one more thing up to "unmanageable and incurable," which they preferred to think he was, because he was too time-consuming and strange to keep at Per-kins.

He figured out the word "cookie" after the first week and one incredible nap time I heard rustlings in my room, and I started down the hall, putting it all together just in time to see Ming twirl out of my room, leaving a trail of cookie chunks behind him. He had sniffed out a huge tin of English cookies, and in his splendid but hurried one-man orgy, he couldn't eat the cookies fast enough so what he hadn't time to chew and swallow, he'd mashed and crumbled and gooed and sat in and thrown over the entire room, and for the few minutes that he was free to indulge, Ming must have been an ecstatically happy boy.

One weekend I stayed at school to take care of Ming. The grounds at Perkins were beautiful and full of autumn. The air was getting sharp and cold, and Ming and I were alone in the kitchen. We were sitting at a stainless steel table near the window. I looked out at the brown leaves and the squirrels and the gray sky, and the stone wall that surrounded Perkins. And then I looked at Ming where he sat, three feet away from me, smiling to himself and playing with a spoon, his sightless black eyes slicing into his round face the design on the F-hole guitar. I looked back out the window and was swept over with that unspeakable sadness which seems to come so easily in a New England fall, and I let my eyes fill up and the tears fall free in silence, and suddenly in that sword-sharp loneliness, there was a motion at my side. Ming had put down his spoon and, with compassion written out on his forehead, was reaching out his arms to comfort me. "Miss Joan cry?" he said. "Miss Joan cry?"

Cindy was glass-fragile and white as an angel. When she was born she weighed two and a half pounds, and they put her in an incubator. When she came out there were little grayish clouds on her eyes, and her parents realized that Cindy could stare at the sun without blinking.

Cindy walked backwards down the hall, patting the wall with her hands and stopping now and then to rock back and forth, shaking her head from side to side, frowning like a little blindfolded rockinghorse. To touch her or call her name would stop her dead still and leave her exposed and waiting.

"Look up at me, Cindy," I said. "You have such a beautiful smile, and I want to see it. When your head is down I can't see your face."

Cindy threw her head back and smiled experimentally. Her skin was translucent and tiny blue veins ran under her chin.

"Thank you, Cindy. Do you know that you are very beautiful when you smile?" and she looked pleased, but she wasn't ready to talk yet, and nobody had taught her how to nod her head.

One day, again in the autumn, when brown and yellow leaves covered the playground, I saw Cindy under a big maple tree, inching forward in her rocking walk, waving her hands all around her like feelers. She was throwing her head back and smiling, and her lips were moving. I walked quietly toward the tree, and as I approached I heard her say, "Cindy's walking on water leaves. Cindy's walking on water leaves." When I got too close she sensed me, and stopped, and waited.

"Cindy?" I said.

"I'm walking on the water leaves," she answered.

"I see. Is it fun?"

"Miss Joan, this is my elbow," she said, smacking her elbow with her other hand.

"Want to see my elbow?" I asked. She smiled and threw her head back and began struggling in my direction.

"Miss Joan, who put my room upstairs?"

"Come on, Cindy. Come over here," I answered. And after she had fought her way through the webs of open air and found my hand, she gave it a tug, and we both sat down on the water leaves to chat.

SINGING

To sing is to love and to affirm, to fly and soar, to coast into the hearts of the people who listen, to tell them that life is to live, that love is there, that nothing is a promise, but that beauty exists, and must be hunted for and found. That death is a luxury, better to be romanticized and sung about than dwelt upon in the face of life. To sing is to praise God and the daffodils, and to praise God is to thank Him, in every note within my small range, and every color in the tones of my voice, with every look into the eyes of my audience, to thank Him. Thank you, God, for letting me be born, for giving me eyes to see the daffodils lean in the wind, all my brothers, all my sisters for giving me ears to hear crying, legs to come running, hands to smooth damp hair, a voice to laugh with, and to sing with . . . to sing to you and the daffodils . . . which are you.

94

 WINDOW SEAT

I sat in the window seat of a Boeing, next to my companion, Ira, flying home from Rome to New York after three months in Europe. My jet nerves were calm that day for some unknown reason, as I sat, thirty-five thousand feet from the earth, reading magazines, watching bits of the movie on Theater in the Air, chatting with Ira . . . But a strange thing happened on that flight, and it had nothing to do with the pilot or the weather.

After the movie was over, people opened their window shades and squinted out at the brilliant sky, stretching their arms and adjusting their watches to the time change. I played with the earphone channels and discovered a tape of soul music. The Supremes were singing "Baby Love."

"Ira!" I said, and began to dance sitting down, clapping my hands and singing along with the Supremes, laughing at how great my joy was over such a small thing. The stewardess smiled on her way past, and I smiled back and then held still while the Pan Am disc-jockey said, "And now to continue with our Motown sound-in-the-air, and a go-go sound it is, too . . ." Next was Little Stevie Wonder singing "Uptight."

"Ira," I said, "this is just like Mississippi, this feeling!" and I sang along with Little Stevie.

After a half hour of Motown music I hadn't unwound at all, and I was in the middle of "Stop, in the Name of Love" when something hit me on the shoulder. In the same second I realized there was a commotion going on two rows in front of Ira and me. A man was twisting his mouth in an ugly way and shouting something at me. I took the earphones out in time to hear him say, "And if you scream we'll send you a pill!" I turned to Ira.

"If I scream they'll send me a pill?" and a stewardess was leaning over my seat saying, "The lady wants to see you . . ."

"Wants to see me?"

"She says she has a headache and doesn't want to hear any music . . . I'm sorry . . ."

"Oh," I said. "Please tell her I'm terribly sorry. I didn't know I was making so much noise . . ." but the stewardess took some cups in her hand and went to the kitchen.

I turned back to Ira.

"Ira, what the hell is going on? Was I being that loud?" But Ira was suffering from a state of anger that had made his eyes fill up, and he said he really didn't understand.

So I waited a minute. I wondered what the man had thrown. A coin, I suppose. It must be between the seats. "If you scream we'll send you a pill." That must be like "Here's an aspirin if you're in pain," when someone is singing off key. I fiddled with the earphones a minute and looked out the window. It was becoming clear to me that I could neither listen to the music nor see the sky until I'd confronted the angry storm up front. I climbed past Ira and walked the three steps to Row A.

The man had probably been handsome ten years before, but now his cowardice showed too plainly, his eyes were too frightened, and his mind too insulated. The woman was easier to understand. She was fat, pale, expressionless —unattractive in every physical way. And in her place next to the window the bright sky reflected harshly on her fury, and there was no warmth from inside her to soften the ugliness.

"I'm sorry I disturbed you," I said to her. "I didn't realize I was being that loud."

She looked out the window and the man spoke.

"Well, it just sounded like a political broadcast," he said bravely, with an attempt at sarcasm. I was stunned again.

"A what?"

"We thought you were giving a little political broadcast and we just don't care for that kind of thing."

I got down on one knee to see him a little better and to make him a little braver.

"I was singing rock 'n' roll," I said. "It had nothing to do with politics."

The woman turned huffily to me and spoke, gazing somewhere beyond my head and tapping her nails on the music channel box.

"We have all the music we need right here" (click click of the nails). "We don't need to have it coming over the aisle. We can turn this little knob if we want to hear music." I started to say something but the stewardess leaned over my head with a tray, and the angry woman made an over-casual lunge for the coffee, saying, "Do you want some sugar?" to the man, who tried to think if he did or not.

I remember feeling a little stern and looking into his face, telling him that I had one question, and waiting for his full attention before I spoke.

"Did you throw something at me?" I asked.

"Oh, that was just a little offering," he said, making another shaky stab at sarcasm.

"No," I said. "You threw something. And it hit me right here. That was a funny thing to do."

The woman tried to interrupt again but I held the man's attention by looking at him.

"It's just that if I was too loud, or if you don't like me, or if you think I'm being too political, you should come back and tell me so. When you throw stuff at people, it ruins the chances for understanding anything."

For a second I thought he had heard. Maybe

he had. Maybe if the angry woman hadn't been sitting there, making him nervous, I don't know, maybe he could have seen that no one was going to hurt him and he could have loosened his mental blinders a little . . . I could even imagine him saying he was sorry.

"Yeah," he said, "understanding. That's what we need—understanding," and he gave me a hate stare which baffled me anew. I shook my head in amazement.

"I'll leave you alone now," I said, standing up to go. "And I'm sorry I disturbed you with the singing."

"Yes!" said the man, in a hurry to have the last word. "Well, you're very pacifistic, aren't you? Very pacifistic." I looked at him in utter confusion.

"Yes," I said. "I'm very pacifistic," and I went to the ladies' room.

I was smarting by then, so I cried a little, after which I splashed cold water on my face and looked into the mirror. Then my mind flashed to a picture I'd come across in the *Time* magazine I'd been reading earlier in the flight: It was a picture of some Negro children in Mississippi. It was taken in the fall of 1966 when the Negro children in Grenada, Mississippi, tried to integrate the white school. They were turned back, chased, knocked down, and beaten up by ten or twelve grown-up white citizens of Grenada. Among the children was an eleven-year-old girl named Cunningham. She had had polio and couldn't run as fast as the others, and when the white men caught up to her they

99

beat her on her good leg with a lead pipe until she couldn't walk. At some point she was hit on the head, for the picture shows her with a fresh bandage around her forehead, and blood running down her face. The caption is "I didn't hit nobody," and all the white men are being acquitted as usual, claiming they hadn't hit nobody. I looked in the mirror again and said "Jesus" for the Cunningham girl, and went back to my window seat.

THE DADA KING

There was the storm of seeing him
Of watching him act distant and fake a regular heartbeat
Of laughing as the young dada king pulled off his crazy act on the stage
Of seeing three thousand people forgive the unforgivable because his magic came out of a well of small gems and an inexcusable charm—
He put us all on. But mostly he put himself on because through his entire dada act he smiled only three times. A bizarre liar, screaming into the electric microphones under the bright bright lights with five anonymous musicians straining in the dark around him. He was a huge transparent bubble of ego. And I said yes to the sounds of his rage and his band and I listened and heard the words, the pleadings, the nonsense, the denials, and I almost drowned in it but came up over and over to

101

call for more . . . and he went ahead hitting hard and steady until he broke his heart in public—and denied it all backstage afterwards —after the show.

Someone drove me home and I walked around the house. I ate from the refrigerator and stopped somewhere in the middle of a bite and waited. Calm swept in from the outside. I didn't move. God was somewhere in the kitchen and I was heating milk and thinking . . . I am lucky . . . The dada king sleeps . . . The bells of the Gregorian chanters are ringing . . . I feel a glow for the dada king . . .

Listen, God, look closely after him. He's more fragile than most people and, besides, I love him. I "also keep the cards that read 'Have mercy on his soul.'"

THE PIONEER

Billy hitchhiked to Carmel on a twenty-day AWOL from Fort Gordon, Georgia. He wanted to see Ira and me for a "little moral support" before turning himself in to the military police along with a statement which read:

. . . I will not bring myself to bear down and fire with intent to kill another human being. I do not call myself a good, pure Christian person, my life has shown that I am not. But I found peace in myself with God in denying to kill.

I have been counseled by a lawyer that this stand may be considered to be disobeying an order. I plead innocent. God's order is: "Thou shalt not kill." There is no higher power than God. Whatever is said after this, whatever happens to me, I don't care . . .

Written and signed 19 Oct., 1966
Billy Wilkins
Pvt. e-2 U.S. Army
Ft. Gordon, Georgia

103

I met Billy at a little outdoor restaurant on a warm, sunny day—the last day of his AWOL. He waited with two girls from the Institute, and as I walked up he was talking and waving his hands in the air and the girls were laughing. He looked no older than seventeen, about five-nine, with a grown-out crewcut and bad complexion. His sleeves were short and showed his arms pale, but angular and strong, and covered with clumps of poison oak. His brown eyes were clear and filled with innocence, and his eyebrows and forehead bore a little worried expression. He smiled at me like a child as we shook hands, and he seemed gentle and oddly gallant. He was cheerful, undiscouraged, and only half aware that he was about to go to war against the entire United States Army. A clownlike chivalry reigned in him as he spoke to women. It seemed natural to him to amuse us with tales of Army life. The stories never gave a hint of barracks vulgarity. They simply pinpointed light on the ugliness and stupidity of the armed forces. He talked loudly and gaily in G.I. movie platitudes with a slight lisp and a sense of humor.

"Here's what they say to us when we're about to go off on a mission, off into battle. 'Boys,' they say, 'we want you to come home alive. We don't want to see your frail bodies strewn across the battlegrounds. No, we don't want you to die for your country. We just want you to make sure that someone else dies for *his* country.' Pretty sick. Frail bodies strewn across the battlegrounds. Sorry 'bout that. And the chaplains. Here's how they clear it all up for you. You won't believe it. Sometime in the first week they herd us all into the chapel and they stand there with their crosses and stuff and say, 'Now you're probably wondering why we're telling you to go out and kill. Because you all remember your Bible. You remember that it says, "Thou shalt not kill." And you say to yourselves, "Is it right to kill?" Well, the answer to that is YES, it's right to kill. It's right to kill because you're killing for your country!' "

I watched Billy's face as he talked, and thought of the letters he'd been writing to me over the past four months. They were teletyped on big yellow sheets of paper. The first one had simply announced that he'd walked into the office of the head of command on base and said, "Christ wouldn't kill. I won't either." He had listened to the inspector general deliver a string of patronizing lectures on God and Country, and realizing that they made no sense, had saluted and walked out of the room.

I had answered with joy that first letter, congratulating him on his action and asking him what he planned to do next. In the letters that followed he never seemed to know what to do next, and I always had an image of him sitting on his bunk trying to piece things together after everyone had gone off to drill. I wondered why no one put him in the stockade. His letters were filled with his newfound conviction, and utter confusion. One letter began, "They've just told me I'm not supposed to write you any more," and ended, "Isn't it strange that men

105

have the power to destroy in an hour what it took God seven days to create?" And then I guess it had gotten to be too difficult alone, being re-born in the dark apathy of an Army barracks, and he'd packed a small black valise and had walked off the base and headed west.

"The ocean is so beautiful," he was saying. "The least you could have done for me was live somewhere ugly so I wouldn't be leaving so much behind when they send me back."

"When do you go back?" I asked.

He wavered.

"He's turning himself in tonight," one of the girls said.

He was caught and he laughed. "I've written my statement and everything. I'll turn myself in here and get shipped back to Georgia in a couple of days, I imagine."

"What will happen to you there?"

"Oh. Well. They'll say, 'Third AWOL, I see,' and I'll salute and say 'Yes, sir! Been gone twenty days,' and hand in my statement. They'll dump me in the stockade for a while. Maybe six months. Maybe less. I hope less. And then I'll wait around for a court martial."

How unbelievable, I thought, and asked him if he wanted to spend the day with me—before turning himself in.

"Sure would," he said.

So we drove out into the valley past the great brown hills and I let Billy talk. He talked about what he called his "violent youth." Of how he once hill-climbed on an Indian motor-cycle that a priest had helped him fix up. The first day of competition he turned in the best time, and the second day he spilled and hurt his leg and had to go to bed for a week. Back on the hill the next weekend he was doing fine until he hit a rock on a dead man's curve and was thrown off the bike. The bike went down and Billy flew toward a cliff and grabbed on as he passed a branch a few feet from the edge. He dangled from the tree in his shiny chrome helmet and black-and-white pinto jacket while the motorcycle screamed in the dust. He quit motorcycles and tried cars, entering a class competition in which no one could spend more than one hundred dollars fixing up his car. He put all his teen-age love, energy, and allowance into the engine of that car, crowned it with a roll bar and drove it out onto the track. King of the road again in his shiny crash helmet, he took three good corners and turned over at the finish of the first lap. "I've been a pedestrian ever since."

The talk always got back to the Army. He told me about his folk-rock band and how it had made a big hit on the base. Billy sang songs like "Eve of Destruction" and "Universal Soldier" and "Masters of War." One night some big brass showed up at a concert and took notes. He called Billy in afterward and told him that he had lots of talent and a good band and not to sing controversial songs anymore. Billy said "Yes, sir," and dropped out of the band. And then at a big USO concert in town, where the brass has no control over the entertainment, the band spotted him in the audience and called him up on stage, where he happily obliged the crowd by singing every anti-war song he ever knew.

We drove up to the house and sat by the pool. Billy looked out across the valley and shook his head. "It's not decent. It's too beautiful," he said, and then lit up a cigarette, and quickly checked his mind for the guard which stood between himself and gloom.

"What's the best thing that could happen to you, Billy?"

"You mean now?" he said, looking sly and scratching his poison oak.

"Yeah. You know. Now." I meant what was the easiest he could get off for his crimes. But he was feeling the golden present and he said, "Nothing better could happen to me right now. This is the best."

And then out of courtesy to me he crumpled his brow and said, "What's the best thing that could happen to me? Well, I could be put in alternative service and work in something like Vista for a couple of years. That'd be the best. Believe me, I'd prefer that."

"To what?"

"Hard labor."

"What does hard labor mean, exactly?"

"Means you break rocks and dump them in ditches and then take them out again and get beatings for it."

"Oh," I said. When I had recovered from the idea of Billy getting beat up I asked, "What do your parents think?"

"My parents? Well, my mother, she's funny.

Before all this started I went home on leave once and told her I wanted to be a Green Beret with the special forces. She cried. Scared her. Then about a month ago I went home again and told her I wasn't gonna go to Vietnam and kill anybody. She cried again." He'd called her recently, and she'd disinherited him after he'd tried to explain that he was doing this partly so that he wouldn't come home from Vietnam in the form of a telegram to her. His father was a Navy man. And so were his brothers, cousins, uncles, and grandfathers.

He rolled up his pantlegs and jumped into the pool. It was freezing. He came out gasping and lay down on the deck. I watched water settle in the little dent at the center of his white chest.

"I've figured out what you are, Billy. You're a pioneer."

"I don't feel like a pioneer. I just feel like someone who all of a sudden decided he can't shoot anyone else's brains out."

He looked amused and then serious. "Do you think we can end the wars?" As always with that question I waited for a sign or a voice to assure me that I was not going crazy, got no assurance, defied all reason, logic, common sense, and history, and heard myself say "Yes, I think we can end the wars."

"How?"

"I don't know yet."

"Don't say that," Billy said, and then he shook his head and looked up at the sky. Of course. Why should he come out into the world after five years as a convict, just in time to be blown up with the rest of us?

"We're just beginning," I said. "What do you think?"

"I think we can make it. Something tells me we just have to make it." He sat up and looked in the direction of the ocean. The afternoon was beautiful and warm, and everything smelled good. Billy got up and walked to the edge of the deck and stood facing the wind. He wasn't clutching at the day, he was drinking it in and storing it up. The mountains, the hills, the open sky, the smell of thyme and brush, the singing of the birds. Then he put on his socks and shoes and shirt and I knew he was getting restless. We got in the car and headed back to Carmel.

"I'm gettin' uglier every day." Billy was inspecting himself in the visor mirror.

"You're not ugly, Billy."

"You don't have to be nice. I used to look good. Didn't have all this mess on my face, for one thing. All these things went away, once. Now they all came back and brought their friends."

I laughed. "Are you hungry?"

"Boy, am I hungry."

We went to a ranch-style restaurant in town and Billy ordered soup, salad, steak, potatoes, and French-fried onions.

"Witness the last supper," he said, and beamed a smile across the table through the candlelight. Then he drooped over the soup plate for a minute and fiddled with the silver-

110

ware. "I never did figure out which spoon goes for the soup."

I picked at my dinner and watched the top of Billy's scalp through his spiked Army haircut as his head bobbed up and down over the plate. I wondered what five years of hard labor, or three, or two, would do to him. And how he could be so hungry.

"Oh, no," he said looking up at me. "Are you gonna start crying and all that?"

"I was thinking," I said, "that I don't understand how you can be so hungry. I feel as if I were about to give a concert, or get executed or something. Aren't you nervous?"

"I'm not nervous. I'm scared stiff."

But he laughed and went on eating. He had a dessert and three cups of coffee and allowed a wave of melancholy to sweep over the table while he smoked a last cigarette. He said that he would miss the ocean and I told him it would be there when he got out. He laughed again and finished his cigarette and we left the restaurant. We drove straight to Fort Ord, turned in at the guard station and asked for the police. The guard pointed to a little green box about one hundred yards away. I parked under a streetlamp and stared at the dashboard and Billy went inside. He came out thirty seconds later, smiling, and said, "Well, they'll take me. Sorry 'bout that!"

I turned the car around and drove past the little green building. Through a quartered window I saw Billy in a war-lit room, standing below two guards who looked down at him from a sickly green stage. He was lowering his black valise to the floor and beginning to answer their questions . . .

Billy was flown back to Georgia a week after he entered Fort Ord. We have a code worked out for when he writes me from prison. If there's a loop in the stem of the Y in Billy, it means he's being badly treated. If he signs with "Love to all," it means he's getting beat up and someone should try to help him. And when there is a tiny V in place of the dot over the I in Billy, it means he's getting out of prison, and no more faded dead green for Billy but forever the brilliant, sparkling green of the sea.

DREAM

I was with a woman who was crazy and drunk. She had on a red wig, all messy and stiff, and her friends left her in a house down the block, hoping she'd be OK. She began screaming for Peggy, over and over at the top of her lungs. Then she came out of the house and was walking near to where I was standing. She had a bottle of bourbon in her hand, and she looked wretched. I offered to help her, and she mumbled something and we went off to a kitchen and she began throwing up in the sink. I patted her on the back and tried to hold her around the waist, but she was huge, very strong, and this was obviously an everyday occurrence. She was throwing up pure bourbon, and it was splattering brown on the sides of the sink, and I said, "That's the most expensive throw-up I've ever seen."

THE GROUP

Lisa sat in group therapy for the first time. She crossed her legs on the chair and looked around. Her shoes were already on the floor, drying out from the rain. Lisa was fourteen and her mother wanted her to come to group because she'd slept with some boy, and maybe we'd be able to say something to her . . .

Her hair was curly and hectic from the rain, her face disarmingly lovely. She was wearing a handmade shapeless dress of bluish color, and black stockings. She pulled her dress over her knees and tucked it under her feet and looked from face to face, smiling at us. She seemed unnervingly straightforward.

The group people began commenting to each other on how they looked, mostly fine, yes, well I've been fine, that's good, you look a little tired, I am tired . . .

"How do I look?" said Lisa. She looked refreshing and not at all stupid.

"You look beautiful," I said.

The Doctor came in and sat down. Lisa studied him openly and smiled. He studied her and said "Hello" very loudly. He helloed us all, we exchanged glances, and ended up looking back at Lisa. She was still reading the Doctor's face.

"You remind me of Mr. Sunshine," she said.

"Oh?"

"Yeah. Do you know him? It's your nose. You have a nose just like his."

The Doctor has a big nose. He wears funny glasses which make one eye look small and far away. He has Groucho Marx hair, and occasionally his socks don't match. Chronologically aged fifty-fivish, he lingers spiritually and energetically at around thirty-five. He is tall, thin, pale, floppy, and kind. He smokes a pipe and has beautiful hands. He hesitated a little at Lisa's remark, made a sheepish nose-laugh into his mustache, and then confronted her.

"Wanna say anything about your mother before she gets here?"

Lisa tilted her head back and thought about it.

"No. Not really. She can hear anything I have to say. Except the stuff I'd rather lie about."

"What kind of stuff do you lie about?" I asked.

"Oh, when I think I'll say something that'll hurt her. Then I lie instead."

Lisa's mother came in and sat in the chair next to me. She's tall and pretty, healthy and intelligent, but can't decide whether to be a grown-up woman or a middle-aged hippy. That leaves her curling her longish hair at the bottom, being a favorite teacher, sleeping with her ex-husband, wearing sneakers, trying LSD once in a while, and carrying a wadded-up hanky in one hand, the way elementary-school teachers often do, only it's not there for the kids, it's there because she cries a lot.

Lisa watched her mother take her shoes off and tuck her legs up crosswise under her full skirt.

"Feet are cold," said Lisa's mother, puffing fresh air and looking very outdoorsy. "Hi, Lisa."

"What kind of stuff hurts her?" I asked.

"Well once I really hurt her when I said, 'At least I respect my father.'"

"Don't you respect your mother?"

"No."

I started to laugh. Just shook my head and laughed.

"You're zoned out," said Adam from behind his face. Adam is like a good violin bow that someone strung too tight. If he gets loosened up he will be strong and splendid. If not he will probably snap.

"I'm not zoned out," I told Adam. "I just think it's great. This little poop sitting there in her gunnysack answering questions and looking so beautiful. It's fantastic."

116

Adam blushed and twisted his mouth around and shook his head.

"Gee, I really like this," Lisa said brightly. "Just sit here and everybody talks about you."

"Anybody got anything on his mind?" said Dr. Sunshine.

The new lady looked at the floor and moved her feet one inch. The married couple looked directly into each other's eyes for a second and back at the Doctor and shook their heads. Lisa's mother lit up a cigarette and took a long drag. I hoped hard that everyone felt fine so that we could just pay attention to the corner of the room where something brilliant sat flopped in a chair.

Dr. Sunshine took another stab into the brightness.

"Gotta couple of questions for you, OK?"

"Sure."

"Any idea why your mother wanted you to come today?"

"Not the faintest. I guess she's concerned." She looked boldly but pleasantly at her mother. "Are you concerned about me?"

"You bet I am," her mother began with an expression of "Whew!" on her face.

"Then why did you let me go and live with Daddy?" said Lisa happily, but she was too sophisticated for that and she followed it up with a giggle.

"I'm just concerned about you because you're growing up, you're not a child anymore, but you haven't reached—"

"I'm not mature. I know. You said all that in

117

the letter. I agree." She was quiet a minute. "But I'm good. I think I'm good."

"I think you're good, too, Lisa," her mother tried.

"Not all the time," Lisa said, "but I'm pretty good."

"Your mom says you been bangin' around a lot," said Dr. Sunshine.

"No, not a lot." Lisa looked at her mother. "She forgets I've only been to six parties."

"Have you ever slept with anyone?" I asked.

"Once."

"That's what I'm afraid of," said her mother.

"I'm not pregnant," Lisa said.

"Did you like it?" I asked.

Lisa lit up. "I loved it! It was beautiful. Really a beautiful thing. And that's it. I can't tell mother about it."

"Why not?"

"Well I can't talk to her like a friend because she's my mother."

"Why can't you talk to her like your mother?"

"Makes me feel funny."

"Do you like her?"

"No, not really."

She cocked her head at Dr. Sunshine. "Do you have a kid in my grade with a red face?"

"Yeah, I guess so. Is he in your class?"

"Yeah. He's the big class comedian."

Dr. Sunshine looked slightly pleased. "Is he funny?"

"No," said Lisa.

"He's not funny?"

"No. He does stuff like whistle during the band breaks. The football lettermen laugh, you know, but that's about it."

I defended Dr. Sunshine.

"Why did you ask if his son had a red face?" I asked.

"I just wondered. I was curious if he was the same one."

She intimidated me and I dropped it.

"Your mom tells me you got friendly neighbors who give you LSD," said Dr. Sunshine. "Is that true?"

"They didn't give it to us. Dede and I found it in the closet and we just took it. It was a good trip. I learned a lot on that trip."

"What did you learn?"

"Oh, this dumb competition thing with boys. I used to compete all the time, to get the boys interested in me, you know, even just as friends. Now it's a big relief. I just don't feel like competing."

"What did your father say when he found out you'd slept with somebody?"

"He said, 'Is it true?' and I said, 'Yes' and he said, 'Was it So-and-so?' and I said, 'No, it was So-and-so' and he said 'OK.' "

Lisa looked around the room at us.

"Everybody's looking at me," she said to Dr. Sunshine.

"They are?"

She looked again.

"Yes," she said.

"I think it's because they're impressed," said Dr. Sunshine.

Lisa was holding her ground with ease—it never occurred to her to do otherwise. She was pleasant enough, though I don't think we were very interesting to her. She, on the other hand, was fascinating.

Dr. Sunshine was peering around through his lenses. His hands were doing "this is the church, this is the steeple" and the steeple was teetering back and forth. He hadn't lit up his pipe, and I took that to mean he was interested.

"You do OK in school?" he asked.

"I do OK. I don't work up to capacity."

"Get good grades?"

"B's and stuff, not what I could be getting."

Adam got interested when he heard the word "grades." He relates to grades.

"Could you get better grades?" said Adam, turning to face her and bracing his shoulders for the answer.

"Yeah, if I weren't so lazy."

Adam shrugged high and made a very "pooh pooh" mouth and said, "I think that's a big cop-out. You're just saying you think you're too smart to bother getting good grades."

"She is," I said.

"Do you like getting A's?" asked Dr. Sunshine.

"Sure. They're nice when they come along. Show 'em to Mom and stuff."

My blood was up. "Jesus, it makes me burn when you start talking about grades. Here's this magnificent little person, you know? She looks as if she has half a chance of finding out what

120

life's all about, and you're going to tell her to try and get A's. A's kill people."

Dr. Sunshine wavered and looked fuzzy and then decided to take me on. He told me about how it all goes back to the infant mortality rate, and how in order to conquer plague bacteria there have to be X number of people getting A's in trigonometry. He said that in order to ever change the course of history we had to have learned the history we got in school. I told him that the history we got in school had nothing to do with real history, past or present, that we would be better off finding out the truth. I agreed that everything went back to the infant mortality rate, and that the reason babies kept dying was that nobody gave a damn about them and that one reason nobody cared about them was that the school systems neglect ever to mention anything about life, truth, decency, love, awareness or kindness. He shook his head and said no, stopping babies from dying had nothing to do with caring, it had to do with getting A's in trigonometry. I told him he was crazy.

Lisa was listening.

"Joan's a system fighter," explained Dr. Sunshine.

The new lady inched her feet on the carpet again and said, "Wouldn't it be better to change the system than to fight it?"

What a conventional bunch of nuts, I thought, and gave up. Lisa knew where I stood, anyway.

"Couple more questions, OK?" Dr. Sunshine was saying.

"Sure," said Lisa.

"Got anybody in mind you'd like to be like?"

"You mean physically? My body?"

"Anything. Sure, your body."

"Well, I'd sort of like to have a body like Barbara's," she said and squelched a convulsion of laughter in her throat. She shot a look at her mother, knowing what the response would be.

"Like Barbara's!" her mother said, covering her shock with an explosive laugh.

"What is that all about?" I asked.

"We both know Barbara," said Lisa's mother incredulously. "She's a slat-sides."

"She's tall and she's thin," Lisa said in a calm defense. "She's just the opposite of me."

"Come on, Lisa, you've always been proud of the configuration of your body . . ."

I was confused. "Lisa," I asked, "did you say that to make your mother react or were you serious?"

"No," said Lisa. "I think it would be nice to look like that. Then I wouldn't be thinking maybe someone liked me just because I have big breasts. You know, they're always saying, 'You want to go to bed with me?' and I don't really know why they say it . . ."

Dr. Sunshine still wasn't smoking.

"Wanna have kids someday?" he asked.

Lisa's face changed from beautiful to ecstatic and she rocked forward in her chair and flushed a little. "Yeah. I want to have kids. That's what
122

I'd like to do right now, only it's not very practical."

"You don't have anyone to support kids," said her mother.

"I know, Mother. That's the unpractical part."

"Can you picture yourself five years from now?" asked Dr. Sunshine.

Lisa counted years. "I'll probably be in Europe. I don't know."

"Ten years?"

"I don't know."

Dr. Sunshine closed his eyes and squinched his mustache and said to the new lady, "What were you thinking about when you were fourteen?"

"Well, I was moving around a lot," she began.

"You're fourteen. What are you thinking about?"

"I was part here and part in France, you know. I guess I was interested in sports. I was on the swimming team . . ." She said some more things, but she's hard to follow because she still thinks group therapy is sort of an intense tea party.

"What about you?" Dr. Sunshine said to the married-couple lady.

She shook her hair from her eyes and opened them wide to look for a memory of herself as a child; she leaned forward and ran her hands along her legs. "Oh, I was very inhibited and shy and I spent a great deal of time at the public library finding out everything there is to know about sex," she said, and laughed at herself.

"What about you?" It was Lisa's mother's turn.

"Well, I was moving from one area of interest to another, forming different relationships—"

"Let's try again," said Dr. Sunshine. "What were you thinking about when you were fourteen?"

"Boys," said Lisa's mother.

Dr. Sunshine skipped me and turned to Lisa.

"How are we going to keep you from getting pregnant?"

"I'm not planning on getting pregnant."

"Well, how are we going to make sure?"

"I could get some pills from a doctor."

"How would you do that?"

"I'd ask him."

"I mean how would you get to his office? Who's your doctor?"

"Dr. Zeppo. I'd hitchhike there and walk in."

"OK. I'm Dr. Zeppo, you're in my office. 'What can I do for you?' "

" 'I want some birth-control pills. There's this person I really care about and I think I'll be wanting to sleep with him. So I'd like to be safe.' "

" 'How old are you?' "

" 'Fourteen.' "

" 'Oh, well, I can't give you pills without your parent's consent. What do you want me to do? Shall I call your mom?' "

" 'Sure. No harm in trying.' "

Dr. Sunshine picked up the imaginary receiver and turned to Lisa's mother.

" 'Hello? Lisa's mother? This is Dr. Zeppo. Lisa's in my office and she wants me to give her some birth-control pills but we need your permission first. What do you say?' "

" 'Oh, well, Lisa's only fourteen, and I don't know if she's ready for that kind of responsibility . . . and I sure don't trust those pills . . .' "

" 'Well, it's your decision. She says she may be sleeping with someone . . . What do you say?' "

" 'Those pills aren't entirely foolproof, especially those new ones . . .' "

" 'Well we just happen to have some of the old-fashioned kind, the really good ones, how 'bout it?' "

" 'Um, no.' "

" 'OK. Bye.' "

He leaned back toward Lisa. " 'She says you don't have her permission. What are you going to do about it?' "

" 'I guess I'll have to get them from Dede. She'll get them for me. I can figure out how to use them. Or else I'll just, what is it, five days after your period begins . . . I think I can figure it out. I don't think I'll get pregnant.' "

Dr. Sunshine picked up the imaginary phone again. " 'Lisa says she can get ahold of the pills. She doesn't think she'll get pregnant. Wanna change your mind?' "

Lisa's mother sounded whiny. " 'I think Lisa and I better have a talk. This is an important

125

thing and I don't feel prepared to answer it right now, especially not over the phone . . .' "

Lisa was fading a little. She looked restless when her mother talked. She was thinking: Babies, mothers, grades, pills, Lisa. Blue dress, brown hair, walk in the rain, Swedish boy, hold hands, fall in love, Heavens explode, no more virginity. Rain comes down, no sadness, only joy. It's a problem. A big tender problem with veins running through it, and I don't know how to solve it.

Dr. Sunshine had his eyes shut again and his forehead was all scrunched together. "How 'bout if I say, 'Don't sleep with anyone till you're seventeen?' "

"No," said Lisa most certainly, and with a touch of boredom. "I don't like the sound of that."

"How about, 'Don't get pregnant!' "

"That sounds better. I think that might work," she said, but she was shifting around in her chair, her feet had flopped onto the rug and her head was lolling from side to side. "No," she said. "It would work better if someone I knew said it. Someone I trusted. It would work if Sam Mercer told me."

Her mother laughed at her nervously. "Oh, Lisa, honestly. Sam Mercer."

"He's the one who made me promise to be straight when I lost my virginity," Lisa continued. "I nearly messed up a couple of times when I was drunk, and then I remembered and just stopped. I'm glad of it, too." Lisa put her head back and sighed. It was getting dark out and the rain was still splattering on the sky-light.

One thing about Dr. Sunshine. He listens to things like rain on a silent room.

"Wanna come back to group?" he said quietly after about a minute.

Lisa laughed a little. "I don't think I need therapy, if that's what you mean."

"Wanna come back anyway?"

"Sure, I'll come back if you'd like," said Lisa.

ORANGE POPPIES

That's nice, when a five-year-old comes in off the hill in the morning, before the sun has burned away the mist, and she's carrying a jagged fistful of orange poppies . . .

And all the walk her own idea.

And all the poppies a gift for you.

CHILD OF
DARKNESS

I'll tell you what he was in my eyes. He was my sister Mimi's crazy husband, a mystical child of darkness—blatantly ambitious, lovable, impossible, charming, obnoxious, tirelessly active—a bright, talented, sheepish, tricky, curly-haired, man-child of darkness.

Remember that he was my brother-in-law—husband to one sister Mimi, close friend to the other sister, Pauline, and mystical brother to me. He'd won me full over by the end, from a hostile, critical in-law of Dick the intruder to a fond friend. By the end we sisters and many other people had some of Dick's blood running in our veins, and mad Irish Cuban thoughts in our heads.

Dick worried about the monkey-demon on the night of the full moon, and kept a little stash of pot in a cut-away hole in the center of an old book on the Irish Revolution. He carried in his wallet a tiny leather box from India which held a hair and a piece of paper with two words written on it in a strange language, and which mustn't be opened until just before its carrier was to die. He talked by candlelight late late into the night with Mimi—all about the cards. And then he cut the deck for himself and drew the King of Hearts. Happy in the strange night, he made Mimi cut a card for herself, and she drew the Queen of Hearts. And they were close and certain and frightened and "Mimi," he said, "you do one for Joanie. Come on, one for Joanie." And Mimi cut me the Jack of Diamonds. And this too . . . that out of all the angles and candles and king purple and gold and burgundy red and hushed magnificence of the ancient cathedral at Chartres, Dick spied a tiny black alcove, and as he whispered toward it he saw that it had in it, among other miniature statues, strange little demon figures, the same demons he felt he knew by heart.

But Dick's thorny demons of the night hid themselves during the day from the sun which shone on a fairyland of beauty. A fairyland of thoughts and images of swallows and rose petals and new love and the eternal blossoming springtime of another land. In this other land he took his friends by the hand, and strutted and bowed and doffed his hat, and played a million roles, wrote a million songs and a million poems, swished his dulcimer from under a tree and sang and talked before a million people. Also in this land he was a writer, which was not such grand fun all the time, which was hard work and which no one seemed to understand, and which tested Dick as a young man and Mimi as his second wife.

I knew Dick then, in that odd world for those few years, those typewriter and spaghetti years which got a little plusher toward the end. And he and Mimi never went under. They never really thought about going under because it was too much fun treading water. And besides, they liked each other lots, and Dick and Mimi had a most extraordinary and rare capacity for having fun.

Out with Mimi, so proud, so proud, on a dressup night. A fancy French restaurant night —a candles, wine, suit and cufflinks night. After the what shall I wear fuss—after the shall we tie the dog or leave him in the house fuss— "Mimi, turn off the heat."

"No. Leave it on, it's freezing when we get home."

"I don't care. Do you want the house to burn down? Sometimes something falls right down in there and catches fire. I know, Mimi, I've smelled it." (He was afraid of ants, too, ants in the house because one would crawl into his ear while he slept and make him crazy, or kill him.) Bustle, bustle—the keys—lock the door— mumble—unlock the door—stomp—slam—out into the California evening. No, no, the Carmel evening. A raging sunset over the sea. Proud Dick, all handsome and healthy and young and

131

English Leather—planning—planning—restaurant reservations—calm beautiful Mimi three paces ahead to the car, calm, calm. Dick cocky, busy, planning—but then suddenly, suddenly the lost look of a child who had planned to please everyone at once and everyone equally —who by some imagined oversight is momentarily stopped in his tracks and confused and curiously hurt—Dick's startled face in the red sunset caught my eye—and Mimi, with the quick flash of compassion which you and I have had at least once, and which can for a second, or a minute, or for hours upon reflection, break your heart sorely, "Oh, Richie! Oh Pumpking!" and there like grace with a laughing smile she hugged him and he sprang back to earth.

"I was just thinking," he said.

Sometimes they would tell me about the fancy dinners. Quite simple. When two people dress up and wear amethyst and toast each other by candlelight, they glow. And it makes everyone around swing a little.

A dinner at home. At Dick's house. Yes, I remember. Dick would cook with garlic. Tons of garlic. All other foods were secondary. There would be music. Loud music—Gospel, or Vivaldi, or the Beatles. I can remember a Beatles night. Dick was an automatic host, and that evening as friends began to wander in the door he waved his onion-cutting knife, turned the music up past the pain threshold and began salad directing Mimi. Mimi made exasperation faces as she began to labor over the greens.

132

The house was at a low rumble. No mustard. Over the Beatles everyone must understand no mustard. Dick would die in a flash from mustard allergy. Simply clog up somewhere in the pipes and smother to death. Someone poured the wine and more guests came and the house was heavy with spice smells. Small talk about Carmel and big talk about Vietnam. Carmel had been beautiful that day and Johnson was a monster and had terrible-looking ears. Also, shouted Dick, he prayed on Sundays and killed Orientals all week and that was pretty revolting by itself. Everyone agreed. One more round of wine and a record change and dinner was on. A last guest knocked and was admitted. He was new. A glass for the new guest. Bring him to the table. Hello, hi, hi, groovy, sit down. And that night the new guest said it by chance. There was always an opening line. The new guest, by chance, over the clapping and stomping of the Birmingham Back Home Gospel Choir, offered unwittingly, "It's been a splendid day . . ."

"Yes!" said Dick. "A splendid day. Splendid. Splendid day for grouse!"

And he raised his wine glass high to the roars of laughter. The new guest was initiated and blushing and on his own, and we teased Dick for his timing and began to eat. Dick held his fork European style and mashed bits of food onto it with his knife. I watched him heap it to overweight, raise it halfway to his mouth and then pause with great drama. One of the regulars to his right was gulping milk. He turned toward her.

"Agatha."

Agatha. It was her name for the evening and it was delivered in high English. "Must you drink your milk with such an incredible amount of onomatopoeia?"

The regular didn't know what onomatopoeia was but laughed anyway. Dick nodded to his wife and commenced eating. All right. If Dick would be high English, I would be low English. Not only would I be low English, I'd be blind and in a wheelchair. I was interrupted in the middle of my fantasies.

"Samantha." That was me. "I believe I heard you belch. I do prefer my own gastronomical fluids. We all do choose our savories to our own tastes. Eat up, dear. Chew each bite succulently." I burped and was preparing a comment.

"Eloise, you're beginning to perspire. Would you like a Phillips tablet? Would you like the pukka boy? Shall I ring for Rob?"

The laughing was steady from that point on with pauses for eating and changes of character. Dick commanded and directed the show, swaying the tide of nonsense, starring but always tugging at the quiet ones to try out the fun—to laugh. Before a night was over he would have gone German officer, gone Festus Turd from Texas, gone Indian foreign exchange student, gone paralyzed, gone weightless, gone blind, and gone mad. I would go with him because I loved it. It was crazy and it was fun,

and the night roared by as we laughed ourselves teary-eyed.

That dinner ended with a salad fight, when a
piece of sliced tomato knocked a Mexican plate
off the wall from directly over my head. The
house was rented and so was the plate, of
course, so we felt dampened and all gave serious thought as to how to glue up fifty pieces of
crumbly plaster. We gave up, had a plate fu-
neral, talked about politics for a while, lin-
gered, felt good, and finally went home.

I laughed to myself, reflected upon the evening and felt enormously grateful and happy.
Those nights of fun, hosted by the Black Irish
Mad Hatted Rose—those nights are what I miss
most of all since Dick died.

* * *

Dick died before he ever figured out how he
felt about "making it." What he meant when he
said "making it" was the Hollywood thing—
having money and fame and a public image.
Dick and I knew when we talked how stupid
the whole concept was—that a public image
was based upon some truths, some half-truths,
some innocent rumors, and a few nasty lies. It
meant general overexposure and self-conscious-
ness (as opposed to self-awareness) and the
constant danger of accepting someone else's
evaluation of you in place of your own—your
own being practically impossible to make already. Money meant power, an irresistible prestige value, and lots of extra attention—all of

which could be used, almost in spite of themselves, for good things if you kept your head. We also knew the meaning of the word temptation, and what a smart thing it was for Jesus to say, "Lead us not into temptation," because He knew well that once we got there we were all so very weak.

Sometime, not too long before the carnival ended, Dick's wild carrousel slowed down long enough for him to write these words in a song to Mimi—

> Now is the time for your loving, dear,
> And the time for your company.
> Now when the light of reason fails
> And fires burn on the sea,
> Now in this age of confusion
> I have need for your company.

 # MEDITATION

What we mean at the school when we say meditation is really very simple to explain. And close to impossible to do. We mean to pay attention. To pay attention, but not to concentrate, to be still, and at the same time, to let go. To stop rehearsing, stop the fantasies. Look with your eyes. I don't know what is there for you to see. Listen with your ears. Everything is alive. Perhaps you can hear it being alive. Sit there. You might hypnotize yourself into a kind of calm, but if it is by a process of exclusion, I'm not so sure that it doesn't close some doors which should be left open. Don't expect a thing. When you expect something, you will be disappointed. Sit there. Don't smoke. Why must you smoke? Don't thumb a magazine. Perhaps you will begin to realize that you have only this one moment. That's all. The other moments have already left. The ones just ahead

137

may never arrive. Suddenly there are a million places you would rather be. At the movies, on the beach, in a hot tub . . . There are a million things you could be doing. Eating, sleeping, reading, doing the laundry . . . Your thoughts will be about what happened earlier in the day, or ten years ago.

When all these thoughts crowd into your mind, as they will over and over and over, you are missing the minute. And by missing the minute, you are missing everything, because all you have is that minute. But don't chastise yourself. That too is a waste of time. If you like, pay attention to the fantasy, the day-dream. Maybe you can learn from it. On the other hand, try not to analyze it. Just look at it. Pay attention to it.

Paying attention is not to try and reach an-other level, another plane, a higher state. You see how difficult it is just to sit on the ground for five minutes without yanking at the grass or getting sleepy? I do not doubt that one can have a spiritual experience, but I'm convinced that to the degree that it is induced it will be fabricated, and therefore deceptive. (Perhaps that explains in part my total lack of interest in drugs. I feel that I know there is no shortcut to enlightenment.) And it is so easy to kid oneself, because of the way we limit our lives to un-threatening trivialities, and the way ugliness and violence are imposed upon us in this cen-tury: Who wouldn't want to have a supernat-ural experience?

A well-known Indian philosopher, Krishnamurti, says that the only real creativity takes place when the mind is still. And how do we turn a shallow noisy little racing brook into a quiet lake, deep and reflecting and still . . . so still that the falling of a leaf upon it can make it tremble with excitement. There are only clues. He says that you have begun once the intent is there. If you have a strong enough desire for stillness, then you will find a way to it. And neither can I be much help to you, for what may be my most successfully attempted techniques for quieting the noise in my mind might not work for you at all.

Why bother to be still? Why bother to pay attention? At the school, specifically, we have a few reasons for making silence a part of the day's activities. (We feel that an imposed silence is far from ideal, but better than no silence at all.) One reason is that the models we've picked as our idea of men who knew what it was to grow up, like Jesus, Buddha, Gandhi, spent much of their lives in silent reflection and prayer. If you have an infected ear, you go to an ear, nose and throat man. If your eyesight begins to fail you, you visit an optometrist (unless, of course, you are a Christian Scientist, in which case you might often have more insight into sickness than others of us would like to admit). If your spirit is sick, or weak, or numb, or even dying or dead—and maybe this is what the Bible means about Christ raising the dead—shouldn't you at least attempt to put your faith in someone who had a few credentials? I mean if a child is sick, we

139

don't take him to a veterinarian. Why do we so easily follow the ways of life of the loveless and fearful and spiritually stunted? Because it is easier, I suppose. It's not a simple thing to grow up.

Another reason for our attempting daily silences is that the Quakers, odd bunch of stuffed shirts that they might be, have existed as an organization for over three hundred years, during which time they have continuously been involved in peace action work, and have never given in to condoning murder. They do not pick the wars they will fight in, but they have picked the way in which they will fight, and their fight is against violence in all its forms. Anyone's violence. There have of course been men who have left the fold and gone off to fight conventional wars in the conventional sense, but the Quaker church has never given in to support violence, no matter what violence was being called at the time—self-defense, making the world safe for democracy, or simply, a "popular war." The Quaker way of worship consists of silence. Anyone in the meeting house may speak if the spirit moves him, but there is no minister. There is "that of God in every man." We thought that the silences might have to do with their insight into nonviolence.

Sometimes I think that it is enough to say that if we don't sit down and shut up once in a while we'll lose our minds even earlier than we had expected. Noise is an imposition on sanity, and we live in very noisy times.

To me, the difference between meditation and prayer is this: If your mind is ever to become still, you will find that the dialogue in your mind has stopped. I think the attempt at quiet requires a state of alertness, of waiting, of complete receptivity. It would be difficult to approach this state when there is still the local activity of a monologue . . . even if it is a monologue with God.

So. Not concentration, or monologue, or day-dreaming, or analyzing, or any certain sitting posture, or self-hypnosis . . . but the endless task of trying to pay attention.

Gandhi said that meditation is as essential to the nonviolent soldier as drill practice is to a conventional soldier. Christ said, "Be still and know that I am God." Buddha once stood up to give a sermon and said nothing. Try it for ten minutes a day. I can promise you nothing.

HOUR ALONE

What if someone were to tell you, said the reporter, that you were just feeling very tired and mystical? Then I wish, I answered, that I could feel that tired and that mystical in those same proportions more often.

I had been sitting under an oak tree that day during meditation. It was "hour alone" time at the school, the hour between three and four when we are by ourselves, no books, no cigarettes, no gum. For one hour the outside distractions are cut to a minimum and we are left to wrestle with the frantic inner turmoil, left so that the surrounding silence seems to amplify the endless chattering of our minds. That day, the companions of my hour alone were the hot prickly ground, a cricket singing, the big tree, and the wind. "Pay attention," the voice in me repeated, "pay attention." To what? The sweet outside noises, or the incessant inside racket? I would let the inside slip quietly out into the air. Pay attention.

The monk from Saigon was visiting the school that day. He wore an orange robe and Gandhi glasses and his head was shaved. During group meditation, he sat off from us a little with his legs crossed, his head tilted up, and his hands pressed together in front of his face. He looked calm but intense. I caught myself watching him hard . . . perhaps if I could dart into his mind beam for a split second, grab the first little thing I saw, scuttle back to inspect it, I might find a little blue stone that was part of a large beautiful mosaic of serenity. Only it would be his mosaic. I looked away from him and to the ground. His family had been killed by American bombers in North Vietnam. He had to know something about death. It seemed clear, I thought, that he knew something about life. What can I do, venerable monk, to pay for the slaughter? It's late, I know, to ask that, and getting later.

Pay attention. I'm trying to pay attention. I'm aware of being in a waiting state. I feel as though something is going to happen. The inner torrent is coming out to meet the air. It hits the air like tropical rain smacking a hot paved jungle road. My mind is cleared for a second, and now all I feel is my mouth, where my thoughts left my body. I run my tongue over my lips and when I breathe in past the wet I can feel the pulse in my lower lip.

What were we talking about just before hour-alone today? Oh, yes. What keeps some of us so undiscouraged. So incorrigibly optimistic. Like Ira and me. We're always saying that we have one chance in a million of not blowing ourselves to smithereens. There was one girl who looked so glum. Well, I thought, she has every reason to look glum. "Rise above your culture," she said. Then you don't have to worry about what's right and wrong, you don't have to depend on people, you don't have to get involved, you can just isolate yourself, it's as simple as that. "Rise above your culture." She must have read that somewhere, it sounded so meaningless coming from her frowning face . . . "You don't have to worry about what's right and wrong" . . . maybe not, but you do, you will anyway . . . "You don't have to depend on people" . . . true, they're not very dependable, but we'll be dead without each other. "You don't have to get involved" . . . wake up, honey, it's the twentieth century and you were born involved. "It's as simple as that" . . . no, it's not simple. It's impossible. But even if I believed you and thought it was not impossible, you've lost me. The joy has been dashed from your face. You have only strengthened my undiscouraged engagement to life.

Pay attention. Flush the thoughts out again. Clear my mind for the hundredth time in twenty minutes. Damn it. There's a song that won't leave me. The automatic mental recorder plays it back over and over. Something is pushing it aside. Something is arriving on the wind. I look up. The oak tree is quite wild in a wind

144

gust, and my lip is throbbing and I'd like to cry. What is it? What on earth is it?

Pay attention, incorrigible optimist, sister to the monk, romantic tired girl, open your eyes, and open your ears. Get ready because here it comes. Ushered in with a sob, there are words. There is a sentence. It comes on the wind and it crashes through the time barrier and it says,

"You are indestructible."

You are indestructible. My God. I am indestructible. There is a young woman sobbing under an oak tree. She knows her body is no more than a breakable twig, and will not last for very long. But she has just heard an answer to a question that she wasn't even aware of having asked. She has been told something that the silent monk in the orange robe has probably known for years. She is indestructible. Something of her, and of the monk, and of the glum girl, belongs to the always present, always fleeting minute-by-minute process which is eternity.

FLAG-BEARER

"Oh, but it's nothing," I've said a hundred times about a blue-gray mood which has me flopped into a dull sadness.

"There's nothing about this sadness which deserves my thoughts or minutes . . . certainly not anyone else's thoughts or minutes . . ."

Because my patch of gray seems so far from

Yellow, like fire which burns.

Or red, like blood which recolors a man's face on its way out of a fresh bullet hole,

Or the horrible brown of cold mud which clings to the boots of a man running.

Or the steel-black of night which hides all the frightened children till dawn,

Or the colors of all the damned flags of a hundred bright and proud nations of the rainbow . . .

(Stick the flag here, stick it there, claiming and reclaiming little bits of the land of some

146

old native . . . who somehow comes closer to
God the Father, the real landlord, than the latest flag-bearer . . .)

Perhaps the only reason my little gray mood
deserves so much as a nod is that

Though it is not even a credential enough for
a gripe,

And though I bow to someone else's acquaint-
ance with death.

The sadness only brightens my vision of the
stupidity of the everlasting, multicolored
battlefield . . .

FOURTEEN
OLD BUMS

In the balcony of Madison Square Garden in New York City fourteen old bums filled up a row at the circus. In the middle of the Hungarian balancing act someone treated them all to ice creams.

PHOEBE

Phoebe lives at the bottom of the hill. Four and a half, she is a free spirit and very wise, with cornsilk hair and brown eyes, dusty paint splotches all over her arms and legs and an irresistible cheery smile. She lives in a little wooden story-book house near my gate where the ground levels off into oak, dust, and shade. Phoebe's mother and father keep a garden down there and when Phoebe squats in the garden she's about the size of a large cabbage. When I call to her father from the gate, Phoebe comes to the door of the little slatted house, holds onto the doorsill and swings one leg back and forth over the steps. She looks me in the eyes and says, "Hi, you know what?" and steps down over the kittens and past the mangy old grandfather dog and past the outside generator and over the stickery oak leaves through the dust: "Joshua is a monster."

149

Joshua is her younger brother. He hasn't established much of a character to an outsider aside from smelling of bad diapers and falling down in the dirt all the time. When I sit and talk to Phoebe's parents, Joshua bumps around on the ground rubbing his runny nose with his fist and making noises, and Phoebe sits in my lap and pats my skin and watches my mouth move. She's good about not interrupting, and as a result she hears every word we say and usually asks a few questions when we're all through, concerning anything we tried to hide from her by using grown-up talk.

Phoebe comes calling on sunny afternoons. She wears brightly colored dresses and she actually skips in the front door over the pebbles and tiles and yells "Hey!" Little priestess of the dust. What shall we do up here today? Tea? Tea in the miniature china tea set I keep on the shelf that's about tummy level to Phoebe. Today I was typing so Phoebe had to handle most of the tea party by herself.

"Hey, can I have some more tea? I'll just put it right here in this little blue cup. Hey, d'you know what I did with Papa's pruning shears? I took Mama's guitar and pruned one of the strings off. It was a mistake. How many strings do you have on your guitar?"

"Six."

"This is all gone now, please. This is all gone. Hey, there's only a little bit left of this tea, see the little bit? Look at these fuzzes, Joan, look at those fuzz! Hey, this is icky!" I glance over and Phoebe is putting a wet cookie in her mouth. It was sitting on a saucer in the Squirt we are calling tea.

"I think I'll have a orange." Funny Phoebe. There she goes. Over to the fireplace to peel the orange. A little bunch of hair sticks out at the back of her head and her shoulders are all hunched up in the great strain of orange-peeling.

"It's getting tough to peel, Joanie. See? I got it started for you. See, that's a small one. See how baby that is? You want to eat the baby one? You just want me to eat it? I started peeling it because you were typing."

I peel the orange. Someone is coming up the walk.

It's Roy, the gardener. Yesterday Phoebe told me that he was her boyfriend. "I love Roy," she said, and gave a quick sigh.

"I think it's Roy," I tell her.

Phoebe turns into a lightning bolt. "I'm gonna get Roy a cup of tea. Don't worry, I'm gonna watch what I'm doing." Crash, the little teapot is on the floor with a broken top and Phoebe jumps backwards out of the puddle of Squirt. Her eyes are big and looking straight into mine. Phoebe, four and a half, innocent, loving, open, scatterbrained and beautiful—don't you see it doesn't matter if you drop the whole damn tea set?

"Here, take this to Roy. It's OK." And she wanders out into the garden with a cup of Squirt. Then she's back in, gulping out of Roy's cup. "I keep drinking out of Roy's drink be-

151

cause I'm a fool. Big fool. Who's a big fool? I'm a big fool. Hey, can I go up to the pool?"

"Yes, don't go in."

"No, can I just stand on the water on the high step?"

"Uh huh." Funny Phoebe stumbles out the back door and grabs a children's blue and white inner tube. Up the path to the pool. Past the mint, past the rosemary and the baby lemon, up the adobe steps . . . good thing we're in the country, Phoebe, in town they arrest you for not wearing underpants.

* * *

Crazy Yolanda can't keep underpants on her youngest kid and the police came up to her the other day on the beach in town.

"That child will have to put on a bathing suit."

"Iss dere a law?" (Yolanda is from Italy. I don't know how many children she has now, but as babies none of them ever liked wearing clothes. Yolanda is sort of a gypsy, with wild black hair, outrageous ankle-length flaring skirts, spangle earrings . . . She laughs at her children, the world, her critics, and herself. Her face is comically lovely, and with the wisdom and hilarity contained in her eyes she could easily pass for a fortune teller. I remember her one day in the Laundromat, enormously pregnant and messy, leaning over a stiff woolen sweater she'd thrown in the hot wash along with some blankets. No one had told her, she

said, that hot water and soap wrecks certain things, and with all her suspicions about electric washers confirmed she told me she was going back to the river to do her wash. Her four-year-old was running back and forth on top of the dryers, completely naked, laughing, radiant, beautiful and devilish. Yolanda leaned across her basket of shrunken blankets and pulled her hair out of her fantastic face and whispered to me, "Get herr down! I don't know herr."

"The last time I tried to pick her up she bit me, Yo."

"Oh dear, I don't know what to do with herr. She wants either to run around over everybody's head or else play in de mud." I shrugged and pointed at Yo's huge stomach.

"How long, Yo?"

Yolanda shrugged. "Last week. I don't know."

Yolanda pretends not to know what's happening so she can be excused from certain areas of what we call civilization, but she's not dumb, and that whole time in the Laundromat she'd been laughing.)

"She'll just have to wear a suit."

"Yes, I heard you but what I want to know, iss dere a law?"

"It doesn't matter. This is a public beach."

The naked child was two and a half.

"Iss dere an age ven dey are supposed to cover dere genitals?" The policeman blushed and walked away . . .

A few minutes later, here comes Phoebe, dripping pool water all over the kitchen floor and hugging the inner tube to deflate it. "I'm gonna blow this down. Is it already blowed down?" Poking the plastic air outlet, "Mama lets me play with Joshua's penis. It's fun. Do you like it too? Dixie doesn't let me play with Matthew's." I'm thinking, I don't blame Dixie, whoever she is, but I wonder who's right . . .

"It's a long time till the sun goes down, huh? Will I have to go home soon?"

"Fifteen minutes."

"Are you gonna type for fifteen hours?"

"Probably not quite."

"Tell me when it's fifteen hours."

"It'll be fifteen hours tomorrow morning when you get up."

"Really? Hey, did you see Bob Dylan when you flied over the first time?"

"Uh huh."

"What did he say?"

"Nothing."

"Do you know the Beatles too?"

"Uh huh."

"Do you know Badger?"

"Not really."

" 'The Vietnameez people ain't got no shoes. All they got is the napalm blues.' That's what Badger sings. When we lived in David Street, were you married?"

"No."

"How come?"

"I never felt like it yet."

"Have you ever had a baby?"

"No."

"YOU'VE NEVER HAD A BABY?"

"No."

"Oh. I'm gonna go up and take a nap. Will you call me when fifteen hours is up?

"I'll call you, Phoebe."

DREAM

Such a sad dream on the night of August 17 . . . Dick came back . . . Mimi's Dick, who's dead, came back for a day. When my sister Pauline wrote about him after his death, she said she knew he'd be around on and off.

There was a celebration going on. Mimi was picking out a white dress from a row of grand old-fashioned floor-length wedding dresses. There was much confusion. I was looking at suede shorts and lederhosen, and wondering about Dick being there. Christian, the dog Dick and Mimi and Kim gave me as a birthday gift three years ago—whom I haven't seen for over a year, though I think he's still alive— came wiggling up to me, looking so guilty, and flattened himself out on a flowerbed, tummy upward, to be patted. I patted him and said, "Christian. Dirty dog and nasty dog."

There was Mimi, filling the room with the

feeling of celebration, and there was Dick, chatting around with Pauline and Ira and Mary and all, quite his old spirited, cocky, funny, ambitious self. The celebration seemed to be all about his visit—as though it were even a gift to Mimi—because, after all, he had died on her twenty-first birthday—and I was so unbearably sad and confused that Dick should be there chatting like that, as though he were on leave for twenty-four hours.

I took Ira aside and put my head next to his stomach and my arms around him and sobbed and sobbed, and asked how Dick made it back like that. Was it, I asked, anything to do with the fact that he died whole? I mean physically not cut up? "I mean," I explained, "that's the way Colleen's Dick died, and Colleen says he's always coming back . . ." Ira said he really didn't know.

I passed by Dick just before I woke up. He was sitting by himself leaning against a wall. I don't think I spoke a word to him in the whole dream. And I think he was sitting alone because no one knew how to treat him since he'd returned like that, only for a day . . . It was deadly sad, and I woke up crying . . .

WHAT WOULD YOU DO IF?

"OK. You're a pacifist. What would you do if someone were, say, attacking your grandmother?"

"Attacking my poor old grandmother?"

"Yeah. You're in a room with your grandmother and there's this guy about to attack her and you're standing there. What would you do?"

"I'd yell, 'Three cheers for Grandma!' and leave the room."

"No, seriously. Say he had a gun and he was about to shoot her. Would you shoot him first?"

"Do I have a gun?"

"Yes."

"No. I'm a pacifist, I don't have a gun."

"Well, say you do."

"All right. Am I a good shot?"

"Yes."

"I'd shoot the gun out of his hand."

"No, then you're not a good shot."

"I'd be afraid to shoot. Might kill Grandma."

"Come on. OK, look. We'll take another example. Say you're driving a truck. You're on a narrow road with a sheer cliff on your side. There's a little girl standing in the middle of the road. You're going too fast to stop. What would you do?"

"I don't know. What would *you* do?"

"I'm asking you. You're the pacifist."

"Yes, I know. All right, am I in control of the truck?"

"Yes."

"How about if I honk my horn so she can get out of the way?"

"She's too young to walk. And the horn doesn't work."

"I swerve around to the left of her, since she's not going anywhere."

"No, there's been a landslide."

"Oh. Well, then. I would try to drive the truck over the cliff and save the little girl."

Silence.

"Well, say there's someone else in the truck with you. Then what?"

"What's my decision have to do with my being a pacifist?"

"There's two of you in the truck and only one little girl."

"Someone once said, 'If you have a choice between a real evil and a hypothetical evil, always take the hypothetical one.'"

159

"Huh?"

"I said why are you so anxious to kill off all the pacifists?"

"I'm not. I just want to know what you'd do if—"

"If I was with a friend in a truck driving very fast on a one-lane road approaching a dangerous impasse where a ten-month-old girl is sitting in the middle of the road with a landslide one side of her and a sheer drop-off on the other."

"That's right."

"I would probably slam on the brakes, thus sending my friend through the front windshield, skid into the landslide, run over the little girl, sail off the cliff and plunge to my own death. No doubt Grandma's house would be at the bottom of the ravine and the truck would crash through her roof and blow up in her living room where she was finally being attacked for the first, and last, time."

"You haven't answered my question. You're just trying to get out of it . . ."

"I'm really trying to say a couple of things. One is that no one knows what he'll do in a moment of crisis. And that hypothetical questions get hypothetical answers. I'm also hinting that you have made it impossible for me to come out of the situation without having killed one or more people. Then you can say 'Pacifism is a nice idea, but it won't work.' But that's not what bothers me."

"What bothers you?"

"Well, you may not like it because it's not

hypothetical. It's real. And it makes the assault on Grandma look like a garden party."

"What's that?"

"I'm thinking about how we put people through a training process so they'll find out the really good, efficient ways of killing. Nothing incidental like trucks and landslides . . . Just the opposite, really. You know, how to growl and yell, kill and crawl and jump out of airplanes . . . Real organized stuff. Hell, you have to be able to run a bayonet through Grandma's middle."

"That's something entirely different."

"Sure. And don't you see that it's so much harder to look at, because it's real, and it's going on right now? Look. A general sticks a pin into a map. A week later a bunch of young boys are sweating it out in a jungle somewhere, shooting each other's arms and legs off, crying and praying and losing control of their bowels . . . Doesn't it seem stupid to you?"

"Well you're talking about war."

"Yes, I know. Doesn't it seem stupid?"

"What do you do instead, then? Turn the other cheek, I suppose."

"No. Love thine enemy but confront his evil. Love thine enemy. Thou shalt not kill."

"Yeah and look what happened to him."

"He grew up."

"They hung him on a damn cross is what happened to him. I don't want to get hung on a damn cross."

"You won't."

"Huh?"

"I said you don't get to choose how you're going to die. Or when. You can only decide how you're going to live. Now."

"Well I'm not going to go letting everybody step all over me, that's for sure."

"Jesus said, 'Resist not evil.' The pacifist says just the opposite. He says to resist evil with all your heart and with all your mind and body until it has been overcome."

"I don't get it."

"Organized nonviolent resistance. Gandhi. He organized the Indians for nonviolent resistance and waged nonviolent war against the British until he'd freed India from the British Empire. Not bad for a first try, don't you think?"

"Yeah, fine, but he was dealing with the British, a civilized people. We're not."

"Not a civilized people?"

"Not dealing with a civilized people. You just try some of that stuff on the Russians."

"You mean the Chinese, don't you?"

"Yeah, the Chinese. Try it on the Chinese."

"Oh dear. War was going on long before anybody dreamed up Communism. It's just the latest justification for self-righteousness. The problem isn't Communism. The problem is consensus. There's a consensus out that it's OK to kill when your government decides who to kill. If you kill inside the country you get in trouble. If you kill outside the country, right time, right season, latest enemy, you get a medal. There are about one hundred and thirty nation-states, and each of them thinks it's a swell idea to bump off all the rest because he is more important. The pacifist thinks there is only one tribe. Three billion members. They come first. We think killing any member of the family is a dumb idea. We think there are more decent and intelligent ways of settling differences. And man had better start investigating these other possibilities because if he doesn't, then by mistake or by design, he will probably kill off the whole damn race."

"It's human nature to kill."

"Is it?"

"It's natural. Something you can't change."

"If it's natural to kill why do men have to go into training to learn how? There's violence in human nature, but there's also decency, love, kindness. Man organizes, buys, sells, pushes violence. The nonviolenter wants to organize the opposite side. That's all nonviolence is—organized love."

"You're crazy."

"No doubt. Would you care to tell me the rest of the world is sane? Tell me that violence has been a great success for the past five thousand years, that the world is in fine shape, that wars have brought peace, understanding, brotherhood, democracy, and freedom to mankind and that killing each other has created an atmosphere of trust and hope. That it's grand for one billion people to live off of the other two billion, or that even if it hasn't been smooth going all along, we are now at last beginning to see our way through to a better world for all, as soon as we get a few minor wars out of the way."

"I'm doing OK."

"Consider it a lucky accident."

"I believe I should defend America and all that she stands for. Don't you believe in self-defense?"

"No, that's how the Mafia got started. A little band of people who got together to protect peasants. I'll take Gandhi's nonviolent resistance."

"I still don't get the point of nonviolence."

"The point of nonviolence is to build a floor, a strong new floor, beneath which we can no longer sink. A platform which stands a few feet above napalm, torture, exploitation, poison gas, A and H bombs, the works. Give man a decent place to stand. He's been wallowing around in human blood and vomit and burnt flesh screaming how it's going to bring peace to the world. He sticks his head out of the hole for a minute and sees an odd bunch of people gathering material and attempting to build a structure above ground in the fresh air. 'Nice idea but not very practical,' he shouts and slides back into the hole. It was the same kind of thing when man found out the world was round. He fought for years to have it remain flat, with every proof on hand that it was not flat at all. It had no edge to drop off or sea monsters to swallow up his little ship in their gaping jaws."

"How are you going to build this practical structure?"

"From the ground up. By studying, learning about, experimenting with every possible alternative to violence on every level. By learning how to say no to the nation-state, no to war taxes, 'NO' to the draft, 'NO' to killing in general, 'YES' to the brotherhood of man, by starting new institutions which are based on the assumption that murder in any form is ruled out, by making and keeping in touch with nonviolent contacts all over the world, by engaging ourselves at every possible chance in dialogue with people, groups, to try to begin to change the consensus that it's OK to kill."

"It sounds real nice, but I just don't think it can work."

"You are probably right. We probably don't have enough time, so far we've been a glorious flop. The only thing that's been a worse flop than the organization of nonviolence has been the organization of violence."

NOTES FROM SANTA RITA

"... That's cool, baby, you in here for your reasons and I in here for mine. We both believe in them just as strong. Soon as I git out I go back, do my thing. I guess you do the same ..."

"... They wouldn't give me no medicine, wouldn't let me see no doctor. See, I got this cerbicle here, in my neck. An' there three discs have been took out. So at times I gets this turrible headache where I can't see or nothing, and I was s'posed to go to court in the morning. I was cryin' and pleadin' for my medicine, they had it right there in my purse, but they jus' told me to shet-up. They got me up at five and I couldn't hardly walk. They drag me down to the holding room and my lawyer were sitting there. They act real nice when they bring me in to where he's at, figurin' I'm too scared to say anything, but the minute I saw my lawyer I started in sayin' how they pratilly kill me . . . I cried an' wailed. My whole leff side were numb, and it looked like it might be permanent . . . That was the city jail. This place ain't so bad. But I'm tellin' you, I wanna get out. I wanna see my kids . . ."

". . . Me, I came in here for a rest. I bin in an' out of jail for so many years I can't count 'em. This time I was sick, man. I was shootin' up five times a day, and that was costin' me a hundred and forty dollars a day . . . Shit. I was real tired. I took the rap for my little sister. We was in a store lookin' at this suit. It was real nice, an before I knew it my sister had it under her coat and she was sayin', 'Shit, man, let's blow this place.' I couldn't believe it. When we reach the front door there was the cops. I was relieved. I just said, 'Take me, man,' and they let my little sister go. I was tired, man, an I was sick . . ."

". . . You axin' me what's she in here for? I don' know. I bin tight with her for three months now an I ain't never ast. That's somethin' I never do. Ain't cause there's anything wrong with it, baby, don' worry 'bout that. It's just that I don' give a damn. It just don' interest me. At first it did, always goin' round all nuts to find out who done what. It's bin too

167

many years. I'm twenty-five. Jail's been a part of my life long as I can remember. It ain't bad. You jus' be straight, baby, that's all that matters. I judges a person on what she's like. If I like her, fine. If I don', that's fine too. Know what a friend is? It's easy. I'll tell ya. A friend is someone who accepts you for what you are and don' try to change you. Simple as that. You OK, baby. You got more soul than I thought . . ."

". . . There's two things I know. Dope and women. A little about men, too, but when you're in here you get to likin' women. It's nice. I got a husband on the outside. I got kids. Sometimes I need a man, and then I go to my husband. He's a nice guy. He's doin' time in L.A. right now. He's got his life, too, like I got mine. We respect each other. Last time I seen him was just when I got out of Corona. I'd bin in for ten months. Boy, it was good to get out, man! He says to me, 'What do you wanna do first, wanna go see the kids, or you wanna fix?' I says, 'Let's fix first, man . . .'"

". . . Hey, baby, come an' talk to me. What you do on the outside, side from make records and sit in? Tell me sumthin' 'bout yourself . . ."

". . . Hey, you the one bin drawin' all the pictures? Do me. Which side is my good side? Git my hair like it is . . . hey. You ever make it with a broad?"

168

". . . Oh, well, into each life a little rain—
That's all my life has bin. Jus' one big storm! I
think I'm gone git me a new boyfriend."

"What about your husband?"

"SICK of my husband. Anyway I got a crush
on Teddy. Think I mon take her home wit me.
Oooo, have you ever seen anything like that?
She has a entire Adam's apple. An' men's
arms. An' she jus hates that dress. I swear,
there's something *wrong* with Teddy. I feels
funny calling Teddy a she . . ."

". . . Whatsa matter, Virginia?"

"Got my feelins hurt."

"How?"

"Just got my feelins hurt. I don' know. I don'
know. I just don' know . . ."

". . . They tol' us you was a bunch of hip-
pies an' weirds and communists, and they
wanted to keep us seperate so's you wouldn't
pervert us . . ."

". . . She the one fastin'? What the hell she
doin' that for? She ain't eat nothin' for eight
days."

"She's fasting to show her disapproval of the
jail system."

"Yeah, well she got a point there. It stinks.
Don' know why they call this place a re-habili-
tation center. It's just somewhere you go to rest
up fore you go out and git busted agin. It don't
ever change no one. What she gone prove by
fastin'? Woo wee, shit! Lawd, I'd be dead by

now. She amazin' walkin' aroun' like that. Some you guys somethin' else . . ."

" . . . Yeah, well, I'm glad I listen to all you talkin' with that psychologist. Because what he said about it's pointless for you dimonstrators to be in jail? Well . . . He's full of shit. I mean . . . well, I think I beginning to understand the word 'pacifist,' you know? I jus' listen. Lot of times I wanted to say something, but I jus' listen, so's I can learn, you know what I mean? An it makes sense, what you guys doin'. And jail, you know what I mean, jail the BEST place to be. Because it's the only real grapevine. There ain't *no* one in here won't know what you guys doin', and then when we get out, there ain't no one on the outside won't know. It's like a underground, you know what I mean?"

And there was a poem I found on the back of a notebook which said,

> My little star that shine so bright in the
>   sky at night,
> My little heart that wanders through the
>   night.
> I wonder if you ever think to yourself what the
>   world would be like if there was no love
> If there was only evil among the stars
>   and hate among the hearts.
> Is this just a thought, or a wonder that shine
>   so bright in the stars at night.

LETTER FROM SANTA RITA

Dear Marco,

A girl just flipped, just couldn't take the pressure of this place. She slugged a 180-pound deputy, knocked her down, slugged the sergeant, number two in command, got her down. This girl is about five feet tall, and heavy . . . a very heavy Negro inmate jumped in and tried to stop her, but by this time she was Superwoman. She had two deputies down and the Negro girl on top, when the woman lieutenant stepped in. I couldn't watch because it makes me sick, but I heard everyone saying, "Hey! You're choking her! She's turning blue!" and the lieutenant saying, "Now you relax, Connie. You just relax." The lieutenant was choking her. They dragged her to a room, five women it took, and left her there and ran to call "the

171

men." "The men" arrived in five minutes with "straps." The straps were to tie her hands together and to her waist. They opened the door of the room, one six-foot-two man and one short and heavy, and Connie flew out of that room and knocked them both to the ground. They recovered ungracefully, and with the help of three women dragged her to a cell. She was thrown into the cell, after having thrown her head back and into the cell door, so hard that the building shook. The men and women had just sighed with relief when there was a great crashing sound from in the cell, and Connie had ripped the toilet off the wall with her bare hands, bare feet, and head, and smashed it to pieces. They tear-gassed her in the little cell, and ran in and strapped her hands to her waist while she was choking and crying from the gas. In the middle of the tears she cried out, "Lieutenant, where are you? I can't see you. Where are you . . ." and I know she could still beat the lieutenant up. The last I saw of her she was jerking away from the men screaming, "Get your Goddamned hands off me, you bastards!"

It's two days later. I smuggled some cigarettes to Connie's cell today. I'm getting good at it. She's on bread and milk, and whatever someone can sneak her when she's in the shower. Her face is coming down a little—it was all a mess, with one eye closed and purple. This place stinks.

I'm down today. Way down. The girl I work with is a complete black nationalist. For a while she liked me (I'm different) ("You ain't white, baby, you ain't white . . .") (She'll like me again, I think). The jail is run in a pecking order. The black kids are at the very top. Clara is at the top of the top. She has about twelve dresses, six nightgowns.

It's the next day. She likes me again.

Right now I want to leave here. I want to go home and see my house, the table in the kitchen, the big tiles, Anathea, the olive trees. Or I want to go to Paris and Rome. I'll never be a saint, Marco, but I'll go on trying. I've been good in jail. No games with the inmates. A slight verbal thing with power play overtones with the woman lieutenant who runs this place, but nothing really. I've prayed some. I love the nights and the early mornings. Mother and I get up before "count" while it's still dark, and take showers and get dressed. I love it late at night when the deputies come around with flashlights and count us.

It's another day again. I might as well write till my lawyer comes, and I'm not sure when that will be.

Martin King and Andy are coming tomorrow, visiting day. There will be a big vigil and "pray-in" with lots of ministers and stuff out in front of the prison, and I have special permission, etc., to see them *both*. I had to do a lot of carrying on with the lieutenant who is half flattered and half scared, and "The Captain would like to know if he's invited," etc. I said, "I suppose that's the procedure in cases like this," knowing they've never had a case like this.

Sunday—Monday—Martin and Andy came to

visit on Sunday. What a day. We had about forty-five minutes in a noisy but relatively private little room. Mother and Martin and Andy and me. We joked and laughed, and King, as usual, was pretty much beside the point, talking about the jail and how was the food and how were the cells, but I love him and I love Andy. Andy looked tired as usual. Four regular inmates, one of them my pretty close friend, flew into the little room all wide-eyed and excited, breaking all the rules and met King. They were rushed out by a big deputy who said, "And you know what *this* means." They got a "pink slip" and couldn't go to the idiotic movies Sunday night. This place is like a kindergarten reformatory.

One of the demonstrators (there are only six of us left) has begun non-cooperating because of what she calls "arbitrary tyranny." She's right about the tyranny, but it is definitely not my fight. It's old Dorothy Hill—seventy-two years old—to be exact. She's not working or eating or standing up for "count."

Father tells me that I got a telegram from Antonioni and Fellini and Rossi. Please give them my special love. I'll get the telegram when I leave here.

"Oooo, Mama. Ah got cramps in mah stummik. Them poke chops is dancin'." Big Gladys is groaning on my bed, crying to Mother. She ate four pork chops last night, and today she hurts bad. She's fantastic. About six feet tall, Watusi queen, four months pregnant, huge wideset eyes, chocolate-brown skin, soft soft loving person and if she got mad at someone she could kill him with one swing of her arm. She just saw what I was writing—said, "Tell'm ah say . . ." and she shut her eyes halfway and waved a super cool pass of her hand in front of her face ". . . and may God bless'm." That's to you, Marco.

Love,
Joanie

MRS.
BEAUMONT

I cried a long time tonight
Because a Mr. Beaumont
sent me a letter
praising *me*
and thanking *me* for the things I do
in my struggle for peace . . .
But do you recognize his name?
His wife
Florence
burned herself to death
in front of the
New Federal Building
in Los Angeles.
She poured
She poured
gasoline
on her clothes
and lit a match to herself
to illuminate the dull fact that
children

children
little children
are being burned to death
in yellow fire . . .
She gave a gift of
her whole self
to remind the rest of us that
no matter what we're doing,
it's not enough.

HISTORY
BOOK

Perhaps there will be another century of living things . . . children and green grass, summer insects and old people . . . not a burned-out planet floating about the universe, forsaken as a windy moon crater. If, by God's sudden grace, and a chain of miracles, a new intelligence, and a tremendous effort, we survive the nuclear age and 1967 is a page in some future child's history book, the page might look something like this . . .

"By the middle of the twentieth century men had reached a peak of insanity. They grouped together in primitive nation-states, each nation-state condoning organized murder as the way to deal with international differences. Between 1914 and 1960, one hundred and fifty million people had died as a result of wars and violent revolutions. Some of the larger nations spent as much as 83 percent of the national budget to build weapons which everyone agreed were too destructive ever to be used. In spite of the fact that violence had failed to bring the things that men said they longed for— peace, freedom (which means 'peace and love'), a brotherhood of man, etc., men continued to cling to violence . . . When the concept of organized nonviolence was first introduced it was, naturally, misunderstood and rejected for many years, its proponents written off as unpatriotic, unrealistic, idealistic, evil, or just plain crazy . . ."

DAVID AND GOLIATH

"What's the matter?"

"Thinking."

"You very sad?"

"Yes. I guess I am."

"What especially?"

A long wait and a little cough in the dark.

"I won't be young when I get out."

"You'll be young . . ."

"Not the same."

"Of course not. You'll be different. You'll be stronger, I suppose."

"Yeah, but I won't be so young . . ."

She tried to cut in on his private images. What she saw was a powerful boyish giant lying on the floor of a local Resistance headquarters, in blue jeans and a grubby jacket, leaky boots and a damp cowboy hat . . . feel-

180

ing good, feeling lucky, feeling blessed, praying to himself.

Tearing now from state to state in a beat-up Healey, peering through hippie spectacles through the sploshy patterns of a broken windshield wiper at the forty feet of road ahead, knowing that any thoughts he might have beyond that forty feet into the future were pure conjecture . . . But holding mightily to some visions of truth . . . Salty charisma in front of a crowd and a clear message of love and how to translate love into relevance in a century like his own . . . How to resist the draft . . . How to create an atmosphere for change . . . How to be a brother in the brotherhood of man . . . How to get used to the idea of going to jail . . . How to be decent . . .

"But this is amazing . . . You're so young! Aren't you making an awful lot of sacrifices?"

What he'd left behind was his role of president of the student body on a campus where people, at their worst, waved colored banners and stamped their feet and shouted, "HIT'M AGAIN, HIT'M AGAIN, HARDER, HARDER"; and, at their best, were bright, conscientious students, unwittingly trapped in a babysitting operation which would mold them into the liberal middle class of tomorrow, as blind as the liberal class of today. That was when he had begun to lose his youth. That step of quitting school had made him twenty years old, and them twenty years young.

"It's only a sacrifice when you are giving something up," he said, walking in happy

181

strides, gaining his sanity, gaining strength, gaining momentum . . . There were others with him now. Three thousand boys had sent their draft cards to General Hershey and were courting jail sentences.

The FBI in December of his twenty-first year, after two hours of interrogation, finally said, "Have you ever aided and abetted anyone in resisting the draft?"

"Yes, I have," he said gaily, destroying the game.

"Approximately when, where, and how often?"

"Just a minute, I'll get my calendar." And he backtracked, day by day, college campus group, local citizens' club, individuals when he could remember . . . "The government is corrupt," he'd said, "leave school, leave the military, start new institutions, be ready to go to jail if necessary . . ."

"You're not impressing us," said the FBI at the end of a month.

"Would you like to quit?"

"Yes," said the FBI. You really ought to, he thought, and smiled. That evening he tried to figure out his maximum sentence for all the aiding and abetting he'd done, and it came to sixteen hundred years. Chances were he'd get more like five.

He refused induction that same month. Rode on the bus with the white-faced speechless boys at five o'clock in the morning, trying to engage one or two of them in conversation by nonviolently shooting a few holes through the

182

wall of fear which was keeping them from seeing. Not much luck. Their fear and silence had frightened him. He stepped off the bus into the lights of the press (the press is always there when somebody threatens "national security"), and they rushed him in a liquid bunch saying, "What do you intend to do now?" and he said "Join the Marines . . ." Then while the young boys were being fed coffee and doughnuts from the Red Cross truck, he told the press and a crowd of a thousand people who had come to watch that he had once been inside an induction center, and he would never, of his own will, enter an induction center again. He said some more things to the cheering crowd . . . about nation-states, and how they equaled war . . . how one must confront the draft . . . and reject it . . .

Day broke, and he hadn't been arrested, so he went off and organized a victory breakfast. He was indicted two weeks later, the fastest indictment in such a case ever to take place in the United States. He was pleased.

"But wouldn't you do more good on the outside? I mean, why go to jail when you could stay out here and organize?"

"One year of organizing on the outside and five in jail does more than six on the outside carrying a draft card. Anyway, jail is not a goal for me . . . I'm not *going* to jail . . . I'm being taken there as a result of some things I said and some actions I took. It's the only way for my body to be where my words are."

So now, the night after his indictment, he

183

was lying with his woman, in the dark, wondering what it would feel like, having his body put in prison for a long time . . . where his words were . . . and thinking that he would be different when he got out . . . These were not regrets, or even qualms. They were just some quiet laments in view of the fact that someone seemed to be hijacking his youth . . .

"Yeah, I know what you mean," said his woman. "You don't have to explain . . ." and she held the head of a very young spiritual monarch, who shed two reluctant tears, one of which slid off his nose and landed on her eyelash . . . and they finished that minute of lamenting and began the next with laughter.

 THE HOUSE

How difficult it will be for me to leave this house. It's made of cool adobe and warm redwood and big terracotta tiles and white plaster. It feels like a monastery when I come home from anywhere and walk in the front door.

The hallway leads to the kitchen. The kitchen is the most holy place. Perhaps it is because of the handmade tiles which cover the corner walls and counter on the cooking side of the room, up to the ceiling, around the wood cupboards, and flush up against the black coil burners. They are separate, brilliant works of art, with clusters of rough gray tiles separating single plates of comic monkeys and quiet deer, and then groups of windy ghost horses and dancing people and then again a single fantastic colored bird and a dark wild drummer. Over the copper sink in a pyramid shape of seven tiles is written in bold Hebrew script, "Nation shall not lift up sword against nation. Neither shall they learn war anymore." And on a single tile in a corner is written, "To Peace, to Love, to Joanie—Don." Old man Don of the Highlands made them for me out of his secret tile-making ingredients. But the most important ingredient by far was not a secret at all.

Often I have felt the presence of God very close and strong in that kitchen. One night when I had found out some terribly good news I was laughing and then crying and then dancing and my eyes flashed past the fireplace and I thought I saw Christ. And in that same second the dance had stopped and I was sitting at the table facing the fireplace, taking the physical attitude of prayer. How strange! For in those days I was not allowing myself anything so naive and unsophisticated as prayer. The presence left shortly after it had come, but the feeling has always remained—as though the kitchen had been blessed that night.

The living room was never put on the house. I ran out of money, so where there was to have been a huge, wood-beamed, majestic room with a high arched ceiling (a mystery room to me now . . . I can picture it only empty, with an echo), there are grape arbors and olive trees growing alongside of thirty feet of adobe brick arches. And beyond that, toward the road downhill, are apple and lemon and persimmon trees.

Sometimes at night the moon shines through the arches and the breeze rustles the grapevines and I feel, as I walk through the moon pools on the gravel, that this house has been here for centuries, and that I have just discovered it. Then I must stop and listen and wonder . . . An owl hoo hoos softly . . . a cricket sings . . . Where am I? Surely this is a dream and I am in another country, about to open the door to a magic place.

When I open the door there is an air of ancient mystery mixed with freshness, and the smell is a little musty if I've been away at all. The carriage lanterns which hang on either side of the hallway shine dimly with reflected moonlight, and at the end of the hall the wooden planks which make up the spiral staircase slice black areas out of the diffused light. The stairs are glassed in on three sides by windows, and when the moon is out there is no need for houselights. At the top of the stairs is a room. This room has no need of fairy-tale dreams to be magic. The moon shines in through the four glass doors onto the tiles and over the fireplace.

The aura of my room is burgundy, and burgundy to me is the color of love. In this burgundy room I have read and typed, meditated and prayed, sung to myself, listened to music, wept, danced, looked at myself in the big mirror, slept in front of the fire, rough-housed with the dogs, chatted with Phoebe. I've stood and looked out of the big door south, across the valley to the green mountains, and through the glass doors east, over the patio, and up the oak-covered hill to the sunrise.

187

In the spring the honeysuckle droops over the adobe bank which keeps the hill from crumbling into the patio, and the sweet smell of its flower hangs heavily in the air outside the doors, and sifts into the room when the doors are opened. A hummingbird dives daily in and out of the honeysuckle, bombs past the doors with his heavy load and balances on a branch of the little olive tree, teetering in the wind and tasting his sweet treasure for a few seconds before darting away.

In the summer dawns the quail cluck around the patio, pecking at the damp spaces between the tiles, and they dash off just before the sun reaches them, as though its first rays on the mother's trembling head feather were the signal for her to flee with her chicks to safer grounds. The morning sun streams through the high windows and down across the bed. On hot days the little kids tromp in and out of the room, dripping water from their bathing suits, leaving puddles and footprints on the wooden-planked floor and wet seatmarks on the wine-colored bedspread. And the dogs race in off the hill and jump onto the bed, bringing with them fox-tails and burrs, and the breath-taking scent of thyme.

In autumn the sun shafts lose their strength and the sky threatens storms, and the olive tree buds little shiny fruit.

And in winter the rain shuts me in my room and splashes onto the patio tiles and soaks into the olive tree roots and drips off the honeysuckle and pounds on the roof. It seeps through a place in the chimney and inches down over the adobe bricks above the fireplace, turning the adobe a damp brown in its icicle-shaped path. Outside a tiny Japanese wind chime rings out the rhythm in the rain, and inside the dogs sleep in heavenly comfort near the fire, their paws twitching to dreams of their wild summer chases.

How exquisitely sad, these memories. And what foolish agony to try to hold on to them. For they are like the most vivid of beautiful dreams, which, even as they are fading inevitably into the past, overshadow the glories of the present with silly sadness and useless longing. How fine to say, "Good-bye, lovely house. It was grand being queen inside your walls for a while, but the world has no time for royalty now, and I must be off!"

For the fact is that my brothers outside are cold and hungry, and while they wait, luxury sours quickly around me, like cream in the sun. And my spirit is so troubled and my mind so hindered as I try, in constant conflict, to live with myself. And yet I remain so eternally attached . . .

How difficult it will be for me to leave this house!

DAYBREAK

My life is a crystal teardrop. There are snowflakes falling in the teardrop and little figures trudging in slow motion. If I were to look into the teardrop for the next million years, I might never figure out who the people are, and what they are doing.

Sometimes I get lonesome for a storm. A full-blown storm where everything changes. The sky goes through four days in an hour, the trees wail, little animals skitter in the mud and everything gets dark and goes completely wild. But it's really God—playing music in his favorite cathedral in heaven—shattering stained glass —playing a gigantic organ—thundering on the keys—perfect harmony—perfect joy.

Lord Buckley—the beautiful moon-man comedian—said to a cocktail audience, "M'Lords and M'Ladies . . . Beloveds . . . Would it embarrass you very much if I were to tell you . . . that I love you?" And they all laughed. How could anyone believe it?

A friend of mine told me it would be risky to write about Jesus. I'll risk it. I wonder if Jesus knows what's happening on earth these days. Don't bother coming around, Jesus.

Jesus, gold and silver—standing naked in a roomful of modern men. What nerve. Jesus, gold and silver—you have no boots on, and you have no helmet or gun—no briefcase. Powerful Jesus gold and silver with young, thousand-year-old eyes. You look around and you know you must have failed somewhere.

Because here we are, waiting on the eve of destruction with all the odds against any of us living to see the sun rise one day soon.

> You, Dear Reader—
> You are Amazing Grace.
> You are a Precious Jewel.

Only you and I can help the sun rise each coming morning. If we don't, it may drench itself out in sorrow.

You—special, miraculous, unrepeatable, fragile, fearful, tender, lost, sparkling ruby emerald jewel, rainbow splendor person. It's up to you.

Would it embarrass you very much if I were to tell you . . . that I love you?